MY BUCKETLIST BLUEPRINT

MY BUCKETLIST BLUEPRINT

THE 12 STEPS TO
#tickitB4Ukickit

TRAV BELL
THE BUCKET LIST GUY ®

THE WORLDS **NO.1**
BUCKET LIST EXPERT

First published in 2020 by Dean Publishing
PO Box 119
Mt. Macedon, Victoria, 3441
Australia
deanpublishing.com

Cataloguing-in-Publication Data
National Library of Australia
Title: My Bucketlist Blueprint
Edition: 1st edn
ISBN: 979-8-580222-89-9
Category: BUSINESS/Entrepreneurship

DEDICATION

This book and #bucketlist tick is
dedicated to my Mum and Dad.

Thank you for everything you have done for me
and your continued love, support and example.

Also, to my global #bucketlister community...past, present
and future. Thank you for your inspiration and amazing
feedback. You know that life is way too short not to live
your Bucket List. Here's to a regret-free life!

CONTENTS

INTRODUCTION

I won't lie to you; this is one of the items on my Bucket List to complete. Yes, this book you are reading has been a BIG Bucket List item for as long as I've had a list...'Publish a Book'.

I started writing this book while on the EuroRail from Prague to Nuremberg. For the previous 27 days, I had been crossing off another of the items on my Bucket List which was to 'Backpack around Europe for 1 month as a Grown-Up!'. By the way, 'grown-up' means being closer to 40, than 20!

Why? Well I didn't do it when I was younger because I was too focused on building my businesses. Now that my businesses are built I can afford both the time and money to cross this one off. Why else would you build a business, right? That being said, I shouldn't have waited for a 'perfect time' or 'someday' to come around because, let's face it, there isn't one.

This short intro is a testament to how a Bucket List can really work. See, my wife (at the time) had her own Bucket List. On her list was a bunch of crazy things that she wanted to do. One particular item was to 'Go to a Eurovision Song Contest Final'.

At this point you may be asking, 'What the hell is Eurovision?' In brief, it's a big singing contest. Each European country enters a singer from their country to win. It's (what we Aussies would call) 'cheesy'. It's also how ABBA shot to fame. Don't ask me how I know that.

Anyway, off we went to Dusseldorf, Germany to Eurovision. And that was how we created the ultimate win-win. I got my 'back-packing' experience and my wife ticked-off her 'cheesy' singing contest. In the words of Queen...'Another one down and another one down and another one bites the dust!'

At a time in 2018 I was walking back down from Mt Everest's Advanced Base Camp, or as the mountaineers (of which I am not yet one) like to call it, A.B.C. Yes, Mt Everest! I went with my Dad, who at the tender age of 65, trekked with absolute ease. No altitude sickness for him. Me? I got it three times. Three freakin' times!

The medic on our summit expedition told us that (apparently) when you get older your brain shrinks so therefore you are less prone to your brain swelling in altitude and therefore you'll get less altitude sickness.

I took this information and turned it into, 'I'm only getting altitude sickness because of my huge intellectual brain'. Mind you, I had to yell these comments to Dad whilst wrapped around a toilet seat in -10°C temperatures at Interim Camp. Half way up to A.B.C. I would not trade this experience 'for all the tea in China' — in fact, we crossed China, and The Great Wall, off the Bucket List along the way to Mt Everest too.

'Trek to Base Camp, Mt Everest with Dad' has been on my list for as long as I've had my Bucket List. This was a truly memorable, heart-felt and hard adventure. Dad is still holding local slide-shows of his experiences through Tibet years later. I'm sure his close mates have seen the same DVD five times by now. (More about this later). Repeat Queen song now! '...Another one bites the dust!'

I've never had a job. I started my first business straight out of university. Actually, I was in my third year of university. In fact, I started a lot earlier than that. I started selling golf balls to golfers after we retrieved the lost golf balls from the mud in the swamps around our local golf club. Yep, with wetsuits on (because we were all surfers), we'd get in there and get a bucket full to sell!

By not having a boss, as such, and being the boss, I've always read about personal development, gone to seminars and modelled myself on the business rock stars who had the same values as I have. I hope this accumulated knowledge can help guide the way for you to develop your own list of people to follow and actions to aspire to. It's important to remember that a Bucket List is not just about meeting celebrities, extreme sports or amazing travel — it's really about personal and small changes that will help set in place life-changing habits.

This book is a blueprint. Just like the blueprint for a building, it has everything you need to know about how to build a fulfilled life by engaging in (what I call) a Bucket List Lifestyle. I like to think of this as a reference guide to the rest of your life. When you start to lose

your way, the skills you'll develop and the self-knowledge you'll gain through going through the process of building a truly personal and holistic Bucket List, will help get you back on track. So, welcome.

Welcome to The M.Y.B.U.C.K.E.T.L.I.S.T. Blueprint™ and welcome to the first day of the rest of your life.

— *Trav Bell*

HOW TO USE THIS BOOK

"LIFE IS TOO SHORT TO BE LITTLE. MAN IS NEVER
SO MANLY WHEN HE FEELS DEEPLY, ACTS
BOLDLY, AND EXPRESSES HIMSELF WITH
FRANKNESS AND WITH FERVOR."
— BENJAMIN DISRAELI —

HOW THIS BOOK IS DIFFERENT

There are a million and one Bucket List books out there. I won't mention them because you might go out and buy them instead of finishing mine first! Believe me when I say, I've got them all. In the early days of being The Bucket List Guy I bought a few of them. I think it's impossible to go to an airport book shop and not see a book on Bucket Lists. To add to this though, my friends and family still think it's appropriate to gift me Bucket List books even though the majority of them have been to my house and rifled through the collection that I've created. All of them also follow my adventures via social media or through our frequent catch-ups. What do you gift a guy who runs around the world as The Bucket List Guy? More books — which leads to even more ideas!

Unfortunately, a lot of these books are the same. They are mostly about travel. Hence why you'll see a lot of them in airports. For me, this highlights a common misconception. A Bucket List is not just about travel. It's way more than that. The last T in the M.Y.B.U.C.K.E.T.L.I.S.T. Blueprint™ acronym represents Travel Adventures. Travel is only one of the twelve areas to consider when creating your own personally meaningful and holistic Bucket List. This is why the M.Y.B.U.C.K.E.T.L.I.S.T. Blueprint™ has hit the mark for so many people over the years and changed so many lives. It really gets people thinking outside the box.

This book is different because it'll do exactly that — get you thinking outside the box. To quote a popular computer giant's tag line, I really want people to 'think different' about their lives. To get you to think outside the box, I need to show you 'the box' that most think from. I want to disrupt your current motivators and crystallise your 'why' using this Bucket List process. At the risk of sounding like I'm doing a cheesy late-night infomercial here...'If this book doesn't get you to think differently about your life, then I'll give you all of your money back. I guarantee it!'

The advantage that this book has over its competitors is that it's a real-life compilation of experiences out in the field. The 'field' is another way of saying seminar room or conferences full of people sharing their hearts out. As you'll see, there's some deep Bucket List philosophies, obscure observations and some super random examples in here. I have witnessed some people do extraordinary things with this information post-seminar and I've heard and seen proof of some people doing some crazy shit too. The weirder, the more random, the better I say! What do you think?

This book is also different because it will reflect my filters. Filters are what we use to scan the options within our worlds to decide what is important to us, and only us. I've selected and deselected the things I put on and crossed off my Bucket List because of my own needs, wants, likes and dislikes. Yours will be different to mine. I really hope it is. Mine gets me excited. Yours needs to get you excited too. Let's not compare mine against yours or yours against mine because we are very different people who want to experience life differently. I'll talk more about this later when I talk about 'keeping up with the Joneses' and the comparative world we live in. Your Bucket List is all about you and what floats your boat. It's not about what you 'should be' doing. Not once will I say that you 'should', 'must' or 'have to' do anything. In Neuro Linguistic Programming (NLP), these are called programs of comparison. By saying this, it means that I am guiding you on how to live your life, rather than insisting *you* live *your* life on my terms. It's very important to note that my model of the world is very different to your (reader) model of the world. Never compare. Anxiety will follow if you do. In my seminars, I am very clear about this rule. I also outline this as one of the rules later on in the 13 Rules of Writing chapter.

DID YOU KNOW THAT
APPROXIMATELY 70% OF PEOPLE
HAVE A BUCKET LIST THEY WON'T FINISH

My filters will be defined by the fact that I am:

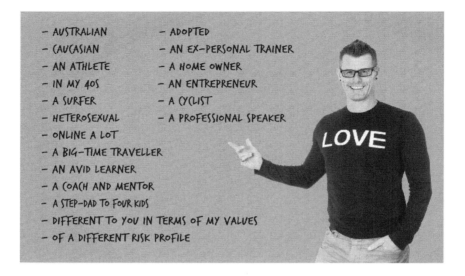

- AUSTRALIAN
- CAUCASIAN
- AN ATHLETE
- IN MY 40S
- A SURFER
- HETEROSEXUAL
- ONLINE A LOT
- A BIG-TIME TRAVELLER
- AN AVID LEARNER
- A COACH AND MENTOR
- A STEP-DAD TO FOUR KIDS
- DIFFERENT TO YOU IN TERMS OF MY VALUES
- OF A DIFFERENT RISK PROFILE

- ADOPTED
- AN EX-PERSONAL TRAINER
- A HOME OWNER
- AN ENTREPRENEUR
- A CYCLIST
- A PROFESSIONAL SPEAKER

So, unless your view of the world is framed and shaped by an identical set of filters, you and I are not going to have the exact same Bucket List. That's cool, in fact it would be pretty weird if you did, but that doesn't mean that your Bucket List can't be influenced by mine. Whether that be a little, or a lot.

But alas! I will show you mine before you show me yours. Please allow my Bucket List and my Reverse Bucket List to serve as inspiration. Copy some, or all of it, if you want to. But please, as I stated at the start of this chapter, choose your own adventure. It's your life, and it would be a shame to spend it living out someone else's dreams and not your own.

ARE YOU READY?
LET'S BEGIN

HOW I BECAME THE WORLD'S NUMBER 1 BUCKET LIST EXPERT

"A MAN IS A SUCCESS WHEN HE WAKES UP IN THE
MORNING AND GOES TO BED AT NIGHT AND
IN BETWEEN DOES WHAT HE WANTS TO DO."
— **BOB DYLAN** —

I first read Dylan's quote on the back of a bathroom door in a backpacker's hostel in Hobart in March 2009, just after my Dad and I completed our first hike together; the 85 kilometres long Tasmanian South Coast Track, and it has been on my mind ever since. It just goes to show you never know where and when great ideas will come to you.

Let's begin this process by giving you some background on me and how I became The Bucket List Guy. (I think this is a cool story; I hope you'll agree!)

PERSONAL TRAINING TO PERSONAL DEVELOPMENT (PT TO PD)

I grew my personal training business to 21 personal training studios around Australia. Doing this certainly wasn't a straight-line process; there were a lot of ups and downs along the way. Some of the downs included legal fights with franchisees to the point where I didn't want to pick up the phone when it rang and didn't want to open the mail when it was delivered in fear of another fight; now, I know it takes two to tango, so I take full responsibility for my part in this too.

As a result, I started to fall out of love with my end-product, which was helping people get fit, and started to feel depressed; I felt that my ladder of success had been up the wrong wall for the past 10 years; I realised later that I still loved helping people get fit; what I really fell out of love with was the model of franchising.

The final nail in that coffin came when I went to a Franchisor CEO lunch. At that lunch were the CEOs of Boost, Fernwood, Bakers Delight and Bob Jane, to name a few. These CEOs had 100, 200 or in some cases 300 franchisees, whereas I had only a few handfuls. It felt like 99 per cent of the discussion at that lunch was about the legal blues everyone was going through — or was it my 'unconscious brain' trying to find the negative? Now I know it was the latter. Either way, I left that lunch depressed and that led me to make a final decision; which was to de-franchise the whole business and put the company into voluntary administration. Our franchisees changed to their own brand and, I'm proud to say, they are still running these businesses today.

Around the same time, a friend gave me a book titled *Happier* by Tal Ben-Sharar to read; to this day, I still don't know why she did this (insert sarcastic tone). I did an exercise in it called the MPS Process; it has three intersecting circles — one contains the 'M' for Meaning, the second contains the 'P' for Pleasure and the third contains the 'S' for Strengths — the intersection in the middle is your 'Calling'; my calling was 'Motivational Speaker'. I told a few friends this like it was some great revelation and all they could say was, 'Um, der, you do that already'. I guess it's hard to see the painfully obvious when your vision is clouded.

I put on an event where I sliced and diced all the personal development information I had learned up until that point and added some of my own theory into a three-hour presentation. Apart from being extremely nervous, I knew I had to do this to set myself on my new path. During this presentation, I started talking about my 'Bucket List' and the fact that I've had one since I was 18 years old; at that stage I was calling it my 'Life List'.

During the presentation, I asked for people to raise their hands if they had a Bucket List; probably 20 per cent of the room raised their hands — and this was a pretty positive, goal-getting group of people. I then said to that 20 per cent, 'Keep your hand up if it's actually written down somewhere'. One person (a life coach) kept her hand in the air, but later confessed to me privately that she hadn't written it down. I was blown away — was I the only freak who wrote this stuff down?

I started reeling off some of my Bucket List stories and people were fully engaged; they started sharing what they'd like to include on their own list. After the presentation people lined up to ask personal questions and get more specific advice, as they normally do, but most wanted to talk about Bucket Lists, it was like I'd lit a fire in them all. One lady, Jo, who was standing and watching all this observed, when it came to her turn, 'All these people are confessing their Bucket Lists with you...you're like 'The Bucket List Guy''.

From then on, I became The Bucket List Guy. As they say in the internet marketing world, it was 'user-generated content'.

The questions I asked myself at this point were:

WHO THE HELL IS GOING TO PAY ME TO HELP THEM WRITE A SIMPLE LIST?

I LOVE THIS IDEA, BUT HOW AM I GOING TO MONETISE THIS?

HOW CAN I FUND ALL THE TRAVEL I WANT TO DO WHILE DOING ALL THE CRAZY STUFF THAT I WANT TO DO?

So, what is a Bucket List? The Macquarie dictionary lists it as: a list of activities or experiences which a person feels they must undertake before they die. As I've explained, I like to think of it as a never-ending list that helps us to live purposefully.

So that's how I became The Bucket List Guy. I built my life around ticking things off my Bucket List, showing other people how and why they should be doing it in their own lives, and then travelling the world showing more people how to do the same while ticking off more of my own Bucket List items along the way.

Now I'm going to share the tips and tricks you need to know in order to design a Bucket List, and as a result, create a life, that is holistic, fulfilling and individualised to your needs. Not mine, not Joe down the road, but you. It's your life, so it must be your Bucket List. If it doesn't speak to you, you won't be inspired to tick it off.

Trav is sharing more in his INTERACTIVE book.

See exclusive behind-the-scenes videos, audios and photos.

DOWNLOAD it now at **deanpublishing.com/mybucketlist**

WHY A BUCKET LIST IS IMPORTANT

"MANY PEOPLE DIE WITH THEIR MUSIC STILL IN THEM.
TOO OFTEN IT IS BECAUSE THEY ARE ALWAYS GETTING
READY TO LIVE. BEFORE THEY KNOW IT TIME RUNS OUT."
— OLIVER WENDALL HOLMES —

YOUR BUCKET LIST IS A TANGIBLE LIFE PLAN

Where your business plan, or career plans, need to fit into your life plan...it should not be the other way around. This book, and philosophy, is about helping you to be more engaged in your life. We are not born to simply pay bills and die.

So many people die at 40 and are being buried at 80. By the time we hit mid-life (I am, at the time of writing, 40 something) we start giving up on our creative sides. We're programmed to grow up and settle down. We substitute living for simply existing, unconsciously happy to let the chance to make our dreams and adventures into reality slip away. While we go on to live an average, mediocre life: Busy keeping up with the Jones's, unaware, unhappy and unfulfilled.

I want you to be the driver, not the passenger. The superhero in your own life movie, not an unknown extra. Be decisive, your journey through this life is like a 'Choose Your Own Adventure' book, but instead of two or three options, you have them all. Where do you put all those options down, you ask? Simple, straight on your Bucket List.

A BUCKET LIST ALLOWS YOU TO BE SELF-SERVING

I have people come up to me at the end of my seminars and say, "Thank you! You've given me permission to dream again and make it all about me". Some people may spin this towards the negative and call this being selfish, self-centred, ego-centric or narcissistic. But on the other hand, I'd like to call it self-preservation for the sake of self-leadership. Not only that — you cannot expect to be able to care for others without looking after yourself — you can't fill other's glasses from an empty jug. Just think of life as an airplane flight that gets in trouble, you have to put on your oxygen mask first before helping other people.

I think this is also especially true for mums, as they are altruistic by nature. With that being said, don't kids want the best for their parents and don't parents want to be the best example they can be for their kids? By becoming a fully-fledged 'Bucket Lister', you will be that example. You're a glass half-full, adventurous spirit who's always got fresh, exciting stories to tell when you're a Bucket Lister. I don't know about you, but I like being around people like that. They are a leader in their life. They are not a follower. We all want our kids to watch their parents be someone like this, don't we?

Someone who shows them that their dreams are, in fact, possible and that not only is it good to follow your dreams, it's vital.

YOUR BUCKET LIST IS YOUR COMPASS

By creating your Bucket List, you are creating for yourself a roadmap, a compass that will guide you to living the life you truly want. It will guard against the noise and distractions that life throws up. You won't allow yourself to lose focus on what's important for you to achieve in life — thereby increasing your focus and driving you forwards. Plus, if you do lose your way, your Bucket List will help you recalibrate, ensuring you get back onto the path that makes you happiest.

IT WILL HELP YOU HURRY-UP

A Bucket List allows you to be more focused and more decisive. It keeps you grounded. Clarity of purpose also allows you to say yes to opportunities more quickly because you'll know where you are going, and so you will know which opportunities fit with your goals and which do not.

YOUR BUCKET LIST WILL POSITIVELY INFLUENCE ALL AREAS OF YOUR LIFE

Every area of your life can be improved by setting your Bucket List and building a plan to fulfil it. You will be happier, because your life will be filled with endless adventure and memories. That, in turn, will improve your relationships with your friends, your family, and your co-workers because you will be in a more centred place mentally. Which will, in turn, create more happiness, open up more opportunities and feed an even better life than you imagine.

Let's go through a brief Q & A to show you how:

Q: How does your Bucket List positively influence your health?

A: If you put more challenging things on your Bucket List will you have better health? Of course! Anything you do which gets you active and out there is bound to positively impact your mental and physical health.

Q: How does your Bucket List positively influence your wealth?

A: If you have more money will you be able to experience a more expansive (or expensive) Bucket List? Of course! So naturally you may find that your focus towards your wealth building efforts will increase.

Q: How does your Bucket List positively influence your relationships?

A: If you experience amazing Bucket List moments with your loved ones, will you have stronger romantic and family relationships? Of course!

Q: How does your Bucket List positively influence your self-esteem?

A: If you write down and live your Bucket List will you create a more solid idea of your own identity and self-worth? Of course!

Q: How does your Bucket List positively influence your business or career?

A: If your boss or business partners see that you have done amazing things in your life, will they be more likely to view you as someone who can set goals and get stuff done? Of course!

Q: How does your Bucket List positively influence your social network?

A: If you go out of your comfort zone and try new things while ticking off Bucket List items, will your social network grow? Of course!

POSITIVE PSYCHOLOGY AND GOAL SETTING

You may wonder why writing your list down is so important. You've had a 'head list' for years and you've ticked some of them off, why would you need to take the time to sit down and write out one extensive list? Well, let me explain. By writing down your list, you are not only creating a clear list of life goals (helping you see what you've got left to do) but you are also symbolically committing to ticking them off by getting them down on paper. It is too easy to dismiss a head list item for whatever reason, not enough time, money etc. Once you write it down, however, you are effectively telling yourself you need to work out a way to make it happen, either in the short term or in the future.

Science backs up this concept too. A clinical study performed at the Dominican University of California, by psychologist Dr Gail Matthews, showed that out of a group of 267 men and women, from a diverse range of occupations, 42 per cent were more likely to complete their stated goals when they used written goals rather than simply stating them out loud[1].

I'm not just making this up, science has my back on this.

WAKE UP! YOU'RE GOING TO DIE SOON!

"I GUESS IT COMES DOWN TO A SIMPLE CHOICE REALLY...
GET BUSY LIVIN' OR GET BUSY DYING."
— ANDY DUFRESNE (SHAWSHANK REDEMPTION) —

Is it just me or does the word philosophy fill you with dread? Does it give you flashbacks to when you were in high school or bring to mind images of a really stiff professor-type with elbow patches? Maybe, maybe not, but the fact is there isn't any other way I can describe my view of the world, so 'Bucket List Philosophy' it is!

Imagine a blender. Imagine that you take the lid off the blender and place in only the very best of ingredients. The ingredients are hand-selected for their freshness, their quality and for their short-term and long-term health benefits. The ingredients that we are going to place into this 'Bucket List Blender' include a mix of the world's best personal development teachings, the latest from the field of positive psychology, sports psychology practices, applied life coaching, neuro-linguistic programming (NLP), Ikagai principle, law of attraction with a big dollop of old-school motivation theory. Basically, everything I've learnt, applied and taught up until I published this book!

So, get your glass out and get it ready to be filled with some Bucket List Philosophy. When you go to drink it, don't politely sip it. I want you to gulp it down fast! Gulp it down as if your life depended on it! Drink every last drop so that you can experience the full effect of it. If you ask me, writing a Bucket List could be the single most important thing you could do in your life. For many, it saves lives. I know that's a really big call. But I know it has saved mine, over and over again.

A BUCKET LIST CAN SAVE YOUR LIFE

I recently gave a talk to a group of people that society had (dare I say) forgotten about. It was to a group of people who were part of a Day-To-Day Living Program run by the Reach Foundation. I'm a

supporter of what the Foundation does, working with street kids, and after I had helped with some fundraising they asked if I wanted to give a talk there. Obviously, I was very honoured to be asked and jumped at the chance to help any way I could. In the group were the clinically depressed, schizophrenics, as well as people on suicide watch. Basically, these were people in crisis, and those who had made it out the other side. The ones who had made it out to a healthier situation became leaders within the group and mentored those having a hard time.

In that speech, I talked a lot about what a Bucket List means, what it does and how you can use it to create an amazing life for yourself, just like I have on stage multiple times before and now in this book. What happened afterwards though, will stick with me forever. At the end of the talk, a young woman, a leader within the program, stood up and said, 'If my fifteen-year-old sister had heard this speech, she wouldn't have committed suicide two weeks ago'.

And that's when I realised, life is too short not to live your dreams.

POSITIVE PSYCHOLOGY

You don't have to take just my word for it either. Most of my work is rooted in the research from the field of positive psychology. What's positive psychology? Well, according to Reach Out, positive psychology shifts the focus from what is clinically wrong, to the promotion of wellbeing and the creation of a satisfying life filled with meaning, pleasure, engagement, positive relationships and accomplishment. Basically, it is the science of happiness, and how to achieve it.

For the last twenty years, it has been at the forefront of psychological research, predominantly because it focuses on how people can create greater happiness and meaning in their lives by being more future focused while remaining grateful and present in the experiences of the moment. This has been a response to the very much backward-looking fields of behaviourism and psychoanalysis, which have been more about solving problems caused in the past rather than creating a less problematic future.

This is at the core of all I do. Whether I'm doing a keynote speech to a room of 1000 people, workshopping with businesses or now, writing this book. This is my sincerest belief, which is continually being backed up by clinical research. By creating a life we are consciously living, rather than doing by default, we give ourselves the tools to be more mindful, grateful and fulfilled. That can only lead to more happiness, and that's what I'm on a mission to spread: Happiness everywhere.

POTENTIAL

One of the most impactful parts of any Bucket List presentation I give is the part where I discuss our collective potential to do incredible things when we put our minds to it. A perfect example is skydiving. Why did we, as a species, decide that since we could fly in big metal birds, that the next obvious step was to invent a sport that involved jumping out of them? It's completely irrational, yet thousands of people every year, all over the world, willingly decide to throw themselves out of planes. Again, and again! Then some genius thought, 'I think I could do the same but off a big building, so I have less time to deploy my life saving parachute' and thus base-jumping was born. What next?!

My point is that people can and will do unbelievable, sometimes crazy, things in pursuit of their goals. A Bucket List simply solidifies those goals for you so that you can go about doing the crazy, but life enriching, things. This is where you find the person you will become by ticking things off your Bucket List. If you have your first 5km run on your Bucket List, what kind of person do you think you'll become by working to complete that? Fitter? More energy for work and play? Do you think you'll be hanging around more energetic, motivated people? Do you think people will be more motivated to be around you?

You will become a leader, a go-getter, a 'Bucket Lister'. You get stuff done, so people will want you to do things with them. That's what I mean by who you'll become by completing Bucket List items. See, on the other side of crossing things off your list is your potential. On the other side is a you that you don't even know yet.

If you are one of the rare individuals that actually reads a book from cover-to-cover, you'll notice a gradual evolution in my List. The items that I put on my List go from the immature and start to lean towards the mature.

> *"On the other side of your Bucket List is a*
> *you that you don't even know yet."*
> ***Trav Bell***

REGRETS OF THE DYING

When Professor Randy Pausch was diagnosed with terminal prostate cancer and given three months to live, he decided to do exactly that — he lived more! He stood up in front of a packed audience at Carnegie Mellon University and gave his heartfelt 'Last Lecture'. His topic was titled 'Really Achieving Your Childhood Dreams.'

He said, *"I think the only advice I can give you on how to live your life well is, first off, remember...it's not the things we do in life that we regret on our deathbed, it is the things we do not.[2]"*

This in fact is the reason you need to create a Bucket List! To do those things you really want to do and to live a life of no regrets. To stop putting things on the back burner and start putting yourself, your goals and dreams right up the top of your 'must-do' list. As I have often reminded people — to #tickitB4Ukickit.

HAPPINESS

Ok, after all that death talk, how about we get a little lighter and talk about happiness. There are basically two types of happiness we experience in life, delayed happiness and instant happiness. As his holiness, the Dalai Lama says, 'the very purpose of our life is happiness, the very motion of our life is towards happiness', and given he's a lot smarter than me, let's talk about it.

DELAYED HAPPINESS

Goal setting is traditionally all about setting and (hopefully) achieving goals in the future. But when we don't achieve them — and a lot of the time we don't — it has the opposite effect. We've hung our future happiness on some result, and when it's not met, we can get pissed-off and down on ourselves. That's understandable too. Now, I'm not going to let you off the hook and provide some sort of cop-out excuse for you here, but there is another way to look at this.

INSTANT HAPPINESS

Have you ever heard the saying, 'What you focus on expands?' It's true too. If you focus on your problems, your problems will seem to grow. If you focus on only seeing opportunities, you'll feel inundated with new options. Now what if you focused on the things that make you happy? Exactly! You will immediately notice that you have a lot more things in your life that make you happy — if you actually pay attention and look out for them.

Throughout history, great minds have thought and spoken about happiness and they've all come to the same conclusion.

Aristotle said: 'Happiness is the meaning and the purpose of life, the whole aim and end of human existence'.

Elbert Hubbard said: 'Happiness is a habit — cultivate it'.

And, Tal Ben-Shahar in his book *Happier* said: 'Happiness is the ultimate currency'[3].

Personally, I love this distinction from Tal as it positions happiness above money. For me, earning money (however you do it) is a means to an end. But, if you enjoy what you do for work or you enjoy the business that you have created, then that's a bonus. Your job, your business and your investments are only vehicles that help you cross off your Bucket List items.

Please do me a favour...Never lose sight of that.

A Bucket List is important for one thing and one thing only! HAPPINESS!

When we cross things off our Bucket List the immediate emotional result is happiness. Achieving a goal makes us all happy. Crossing it off, or ticking it, gives us a great sense of satisfaction. It puts a smile on our face. Am I right, or am I right?

PEOPLE ARE
DYING AT 40 AND
BEING BURIED
AT 80.

THE 80 SQUARES EXERCISE

Now I'd like to make something clear to you, I'm not a morbid person. I speak often about death but I'm not obsessed with it. I just help use it as a catalyst, a driver to push me forward to do new and different things. I just really want a cool highlight reel played at my funeral, full of amazing things I've seen and done, with all the amazing people I have met. It makes it exciting for me, to see how much life I can squeeze out before I do kick it.

With that in mind, I want you to do the first of a few exercises I'll get you to complete as you go through this book. Don't worry, you don't have to read something in public in the nude (though if that does worry you stay away from chapter 20). All I want you to do is follow these simple instructions:

On the next page, you will find a grid made up of 80 squares. Each square represents a year.

As the average life expectancy of an Australian is just a little more than 82 years (a bit more for women, less for men)...you may guess where this is going. For ease of the exercises we've rounded it down to 80.

Mark down how many years old you are by crossing out the corresponding boxes.

Now you have done the exercise, look back at the grid, how much of your life have you already used? How does it make you feel when you look at it? Think on that then answer the following 3 questions:

1. Do you know someone who has been diagnosed with or died from cancer? Write their names.

....

....

....

2. How many people do you personally know who have been diagnosed with or died from cancer? Write a number.

....

....

....

3. How many of the people you know made their 80- squares? Write a number.

....

....

....

YOUR LIFE GRID

	2016 World Bank Life Expectancy at Birth[4]	2016-17 CIA The World Factbook: Life Expectancy at Birth[5]	OECD (2015-2017): Life Expectancy at Birth[6]
Australia	82.45	82.401 (World Rank 14)	82.5
Austria	81.64	81.70 (World Rank 24)	81.7
Canada	82.30	82.00 (World Rank 18)	81.4
Costa Rica	79.83	78.90 (World Rank 55)	79.6
Germany	80.99	80.90 (World Rank 37)	81.1
India	68.56	69.10 (World Rank 163)	68.4
Namibia	64.38	64.40 (World Rank 189)	No data
New Zealand	81.61	81.40 (World Rank 30)	81.7
Mexico	77.12	76.30 (World Rank 89)	75.4
Portugal	81.12	80.90 (World Rank 38)	81.2
South Africa	62.77	64.1 (World Rank 190)	57.5
USA	78.54	80.10 (World Rank 45)	78.6
Vietnam	76.25	73.9 (World Rank 132)	No data

A few tidbits on global life expectancy to make you think a little further about how important it is to live life purposefully:

- Highest CIA World Factbook Ranking 1: Monaco 89.4
- Lowest CIA World Factbook Ranking 223: Afghanistan 52.1
- According to the World Health Organization's Global Health Observatory 72.0 years was the average life expectancy at birth of the global population in 2016.
- Women outlive men everywhere in the world — particularly in wealthy countries.

DID YOU DO YOUR 80 SQUARE GRID?

Now how does the Life Grid make you feel?

Does it scare you? Why?

Or does it make you want to get out there and fill the rest of those squares with all the living you possibly can?

Trav is sharing more
in his INTERACTIVE book.

See exclusive
behind-the-scenes
videos, audios and photos.

DOWNLOAD it now at
deanpublishing.com/mybucketlist

THE
M.Y.B.U.C.K.E.T.L.I.S.T. BLUEPRINT™

"A GOAL WITHOUT A PLAN IS JUST A WISH."
— ANTOINE DE SAINT-EXUPERY —

The M.Y.B.U.C.K.E.T.L.I.S.T. Blueprint™ will help you create a personally meaningful and holistic Bucket List. It will get you thinking in a way that you haven't thought before...I hope!

You need to set aside time to do it and clearly establish your big WHY for doing it. If you don't prioritise it and time-block to do it, the list will become like a lot of things in your life...incomplete. They say that success is completion. So, for life's-sake, finish what you

25

start here, don't become a statistic and don't let this become another addition to your dusty 'shelf-help' library.

My hope is that The M.Y.B.U.C.K.E.T.L.I.S.T. Blueprint™ will stick with you for the rest of your life. My hope is that it becomes a reference point that you can always come back and refer to. This is what it has been for me.

My 'little' acronym is designed to search into the dark corners of your brain. To find all the things that you really want to do in your life. If you talk to most people about Bucket Lists they'll give you only one or (at a stretch) two components of The M.Y.B.U.C.K.E.T.L.I.S.T. Blueprint™. They'll give you the C or the T (you'll find this out soon).

It would be remiss of me not to mention that this sounds like an AA Meeting when I present to you...my 12 Step Plan; The M.Y.B.U.C.K.E.T.L.I.S.T. Blueprint™.

The M.Y.B.U.C.K.E.T.L.I.S.T. acronym was formulated over the years as I found (sometimes strange) things to add to my Bucket List. At the heart of each letter is the need for specificity. The more specific your goals can be, the clearer your emotional connection to them will be. The greater the emotional connection you have to a goal the more likelihood you have of achieving it.

Let's look at the fantastic 'little' acronym:

The M.Y.B.U.C.K.E.T.L.I.S.T. Blueprint™

We start off at the beginning with **M**eet a Personal Hero, which is pretty self-explanatory isn't it? Think about who you'd like to meet, work out how to, then make it happen. No stalking though, not cool.

Next, we come to **Y**our Proud Achievements. What do you want to look back on in later years and say, 'Yeah, I'm proud of that?' **B**uy Something Special comes next, and this makes some people worry about being materialistic, but there is a difference between treating yourself and being a shopaholic, so relax. Your something special may even come from an op-shop — it's not the worth of the item but the significance it has that is important.

The next two sections are Ultimate Challenges and Conquer a Fear. For some of you there may be some overlap between these two, and that's not an issue. More on that later but the thing to remember is that it's your Bucket List so if roller-coasters are fun for you, don't put 'Ride the world's 5 biggest roller-coasters' under Conquer a Fear.

Following is Kind Acts for Others. This is about acts of service and giving back, and I've found that these are some of the most rewarding Bucket List items to tick off. Then we have Express Yourself, making sure you do something to nurture and develop your creative side, and Take Lessons, two other areas you may have to think carefully about. Particularly if you've lived a life focused on a more analytic style of thinking than the creative.

Leaving a Legacy is incredibly important to many people, but have you personally thought about what your legacy will be? Now's the time to start. This item can be heavy going, so after the deep thought required here it is followed up with Idiotic Stuff. This is the crazy uncle of the Bucket List family, undoubtedly weird but guaranteed to give you some great stories. Just maybe don't tell Nanna.

Satisfy a Curiosity can be also be weird but also an expansive part of your Bucket List, as it does cover literally everything you've thought 'I wonder...' about.

Finally, we have the Bucket List area that most of you will be at least somewhat prepared to write, Travel Adventures. This is what people usually first think of when they think Bucket List.

Don't worry if those quick explanations seemed a bit brief. In the next few chapters, we'll go through the whole M.Y.B.U.C.K.E.T.L.I.S.T. Blueprint™ in more detail and I'll give you an example of my own experiences ticking things off, as well as real world stories of people who have followed the blueprint to create their own Bucket List and then gone out and made it happen. I've also included at the end of each chapter my Bucket List for this section, the matching Reverse

Bucket List and suggestions for some things you could add to your Bucket List.

As you will see, there is so much more to a holistic and personal Bucket List than just 'Climb Everest, Walk the Camino de Santiago de Compostela, and Eat Snails'. These are all worthy and exciting experiences, but if they don't speak to you, why bother? This process is designed to help you be more aware of what you want out of life, develop the traits needed to make these things happen and live a happier life because you are designing it, rather than being at the mercy of the whims of others. Living a purpose filled life driven by gratitude is the key to ongoing happiness. Being content with your 'now' allows you to strive for the future with defined clarity.

YOUR REVERSE BUCKET LIST (RBL)

We all have just one life to live
How long we have is unsure
But how we play the game of life
Can determine so much more

Like if we get to the end of it
and wished that we'd done more
Like regretting not making that bucketlist
and ticking it off to be sure

Now the answer to this list, you may think
is about all the places you must travel
But let me tell you a secret
My list gives you much more to unravel

What matters in life is how you live
And if you leave it a better place
It's how you connect with others
We're all from the one human race

It's the things we put on our list
That help us enjoy our lifetime
Crazy, wonderful, sometimes scary things
And cross them off one at a time

It is how we show up in life
How we give back and lead
Whether it is feeding the poor
Or simply planting a seed

Whether it's running a marathon
Or granting someone's dying wish
Buying a kayak or a new car
Or swimming with large-prey fish

It could be leaving a legacy
like writing a book
Or the hero you met
Whose photo you took

Whether it's a moment you're proud of
Because you conquered a fear
A challenge you overcome
Like skydiving from earth's atmosphere

There are so many things we can do
To enjoy the gift we all have
After all - we only have one life
So live fully the one you that you have

So smile and love
And squeeze every bit
Dance freely and laugh
'Til your aching sides split

Give it your best
Make it all count
Tick all the boxes
Till they take your box out.

Your to-do lists will fade
But your bucketlist gives
So 'Tick it B4 U Kick it'.
Is the only way to live.

WHAT IS A REVERSE BUCKET LIST (RBL)?

Let's talk about funerals. Yes, it's morbid I know but stay with me here. There are 3 things that happen at funerals. They are:

- Your friends and family turn up to show you respect. These include the people that you have attracted into your life.
- Your character is discussed. These are the things that you stood for.
- Your Reverse Bucket List is played out. The YouTube Generation may show a visual representation through video documentary of how you lived your life.

It's this last one that I want to concentrate on now. Bucket Lists for some people are a wish list, a dream list or a 'someday' list. A Reverse Bucket List is all the things you have done on your Bucket List. Just as a Bucket List is your TO DO List, your Reverse Bucket List is your DONE List.

WHY COMPLETE A REVERSE BUCKET LIST (RBL)?

Before we even get started on a Bucket List, I want you to think about your Reverse Bucket List. Think back through your life and consider all the things you've done. Think about it as if you had had a Bucket List all along. What have you done that you would have had on that hypothetical list? That's the start of your Reverse Bucket List. In the space at the end of this chapter, I want you to start writing those things down. No matter what they are, if you think they would have been on your Bucket List, or if you had what I call a Brain Bucket List that you've ticked off then write them down.

Then I want you to make a Reverse Bucket List Board. This is a visual reminder of all the awesome things you've done, the great memories, the cool lessons, the valuable moments you made happen with and for people. Put them all on there and put it up somewhere you're going to see it regularly. I want you to be reminded by yourself about the great things you have already accomplished.

Think of this as both a motivational and gratitude exercise. It'll be motivational because you'll want to add more things to the board, and its gratitude inducing as it will help you remain appreciative of the good things in life you've already experienced. Seeing both your Reverse Bucket List, and eventually your Future Bucket List, as visual representations of your plans will also strengthen your emotional connection to making these things happen. Reminding you to keep living your life by design, not by default.

I am going to list my Reverse Bucket List items (the ones that I've done) as part of each section so that it adds inspiration to the Bucket List that you are creating in this book. I'm going to show you mine if you show me yours...so to speak!

Most audience members I speak to don't have a documented, written down Bucket List. When I ask them to raise their hand after the question, 'Who here has a Bucket List written down?', I'm constantly reassured that I'm in a job for life. When I ask audiences to list 5 things they've done in their life as if those things were on a Bucket List all the way along, most struggle. I bring it back to just 3 things.

We live in a world where we're always looking forwards toward the next goal, not backwards. Positive psychology teaches us to be more mindful, present and show more gratitude. Doing this allows us to celebrate our lives more and recognise what we have done. Doing this reduces anxiety and gives us space to be happier.

As you will see, I created the M.Y.B.U.C.K.E.T.L.I.S.T. Blueprint™ to help prompt your memories. Going through this on the pages ahead will really help you go north, south, east and west in your brain and help you to extract these memories for your Reverse Bucket List.

YOUR REVERSE BUCKET LIST

Write it down here. Claim your past achievements. For every letter of M.Y.B.U.C.K.E.T.L.I.S.T. think of something in your past that you have done that's worth remembering and celebrating. I would love you to share it with me, The Bucket List Guy, at https://thebucketlistguy.com/upload-your-list

M   **MEET A PERSONAL HERO**

Y   **YOUR PROUD ACHIEVEMENTS**

BUY THAT SPECIAL SOMETHING

ULTIMATE CHALLENGES

CONQUER A FEAR

KIND ACTS FOR OTHERS

EXPRESS YOURSELF

TAKE LESSONS

LEAVE A LEGACY ....

....

....

....

....

....

....

IDIOTIC STUFF ....

....

....

....

....

....

....

SATISFY A CURIOSITY ....

....

....

....

....

....

....

TRAVEL ADVENTURES

YOUR FUTURE
BUCKET LIST (FBL)

"ONE DAY YOUR LIFE WILL FLASH BEFORE YOUR EYES.
MAKE SURE IT'S WORTH WATCHING."
— THE BUCKET LIST MOVIE 2007 —

WHAT IS A FUTURE BUCKET LIST (FBL)?

Your Future Bucket List is your To Do List. As opposed to your Reverse Bucket List, which is your Done List. It's all the cool things you want to do in your life. From the things you want, the people you want to meet, the experiences you want to experience, the challenges you want to overcome, the fears you want to overcome, the places you want to go, and the kind acts you want to pay forward to others.

39

WHY DO A FUTURE BUCKET LIST (FBL)?

Why not do a Future Bucket List, I say! It is essential to separate your daily To Do List from your Bucket List. Because both lists are swimming around in your head and guess which one gets done first? That's right...your daily To Do List. But, it's only when something traumatic or dramatic happens to you or a loved one that you shift priorities.

Unfortunately, it's sad that, as human beings, normally, we need such an emotional slap to get us to reprioritise. But humans will be humans. We are so busy being busy. It's like this weird badge of honour we use in conversation these days. You've probably seen the meme...'Are we here to just pay bills and die?'

As you will see, I created the M.Y.B.U.C.K.E.T.L.I.S.T. Blueprint™ to prompt people to go to places in their mind that they've never been before. Additionally, it helps to bring back past dreams that people may have forgotten. It's a big unearthing process for most. For some, it adds icing on the cake to what is already an amazing life. See this as a new filter through which to look at your life. This will help you, as it has for hundreds of thousands already, create a personally meaningful and holistic Bucket List. It's one thing to think about this stuff. It's another to write it down. Going through this on the pages ahead will really help you articulate your list on a whole new level.

RULES OF WRITING

1. ALLOW CATEGORY CROSS-OVER

"I grew up in a wonderful blend of a lot of old culture."
Kenny Ortega

Bucket Listers, you may find yourself reading the examples that I have placed under each acronym and thinking that there is a lot of overlapping in varying categories. This is fundamentally inevitable; as everyone of us can, and will, perceive each example in a completely personal manner. When creating a holistic and meaningful Bucket List, you should remember it is just that. You must write one that is extremely personal and meaningful to you, the reader, the Bucket Lister!

I have placed 'Running with the bulls at the Fiestas of San Fermin in Pamplona, Spain' under 'Satisfy a Curiosity'. Now I'm sure this example can certainly be seen as overlapping across a few categories for other Bucket Listers, as it did for me. Using this as an example, I could have easily placed this under various categories. You may find yourself thinking, yes this is on my list too, however it's on my Bucket List under 'Conquer a Fear', or 'Travel Adventure' or even, 'Idiotic Stuff'.

Another example that I have had written down on my Bucket List for many years which I have placed under 'Conquering a Fear' is to perform a stand-up comedy gig. Placing this under this section of the acronym is purely personal for me, as once I've crossed this off my list, I know I would have conquered a fear of mine that has been lurking for some time. And naturally I'm hoping along with this being ticked off, it will be well received with lots of laughs too! Having the same Bucket List item written down on your own Bucket List may very well come under another category such as 'Express Yourself', 'Satisfy a Curiosity' or once again just fall under, 'Idiotic Stuff'.

Climbing Mount Kilimanjaro is another prime example of doubling up, or crossing over, for me. I put this under 'Ultimate Challenge'. The reasoning for this was that I had personally spent five gruelling days climbing this beast, and finally reached the summit on day 6! I was physically exhausted, sleep deprived, suffering from severe altitude sickness, not to mention having far too many blisters! Yet for one of my fellow Bucket Listers reading this, they could easily have this under another category/another letter of the acronym. This could be more personal for you under 'Leaving a Legacy' or this challenge could be part of something bigger — climbing this mountain for you could be to help raise awareness and funds for a foundation that is very close to your heart. Or this could easily come under the T part of the acronym; 'Travel Adventures' for others; as climbing Mount Kilimanjaro simply may be more about the fact that it means travelling to Tanzania.

Whichever category/part of the acronym you decide to place your goals in, remember that some aspirations, dreams, goals you have set yourself may very well overlap into various acronyms which just makes them even more meaningful, and more fun!

The main purpose of writing down your own meaningful and holistic Bucket List is to truly stretch yourself to reach your full potential. As The Bucket List Guy, I am always striving to be the best version of myself. My mission in life which falls under 'Leave a Legacy' is that I wish to pay this forward to everyone I meet. For you all to live a life of no regrets, as life is just way too short not to live your Bucket List.

2. CREATE A BUCKET LIST SNOWBALL

"We live in a world of cause and effect."
T. Harv Eker

Once you start moving things from your Future Bucket List to your Reverse Bucket List, you will not want to stop. So, get on with it! Start small, do the easiest ones that don't take a lot of time and money first. Then move onto the bigger ones. The snowball effect of getting the easy ones out of the way quickly will drive your motivation onwards and upwards. You've got to create momentum.

3. COMBINE INSTANT AND DELAYED GRATIFICATION

"Little by little, a little becomes a lot."
Tanzanian Proverb

The whole point of this is to be able to start straight away, so combine some immediate (in the next month), some short term (the next year) and some longer-term items (years to come). Once you get moving in the process, your momentum will build, and you'll find yourself doing bigger and bigger list items in no time.

Designing a list that gives you some instant and some delayed gratification also helps give you a taste of the joy of ticking off a Bucket List item without having to wait too long.

4. GOT TO BE ECOLOGICAL

"Take care, be kind, be considerate of other people and other species, and be loving."
John Lithgow

There is no point setting up a Bucket List if on the first outing you are likely to get killed or severely injured. Take risks, that's fine, just be aware of what you are doing, do the right preparation and make sure you are still alive at the end of it to be able to tick it off your list. Otherwise what's the point? You can't tell a great story if you're 6ft under. This goes for other people and the environment too. Just be good to yourself, other people and the planet while you're Bucket Listing. Simple.

5. THE MORE SPECIFIC THE BETTER

"I have discovered that you achieve nothing if you pursue everything. Be specific and stay focused."
Israelmore Ayivor

You'll notice that the examples I've given you are very specific. They are not generalised statements. You need to be as specific as you can with listing items. That will help you picture the experience before it happens, and that excitement will keep pushing you on to tick off more and more.

6. THE MORE RANDOM THE BETTER

"Some quotations...are greatly improved by lack of context."
John Wyndam

Get weird with this. Why shouldn't you? It's your list. If you want to ride from Melbourne to Mackay on a skateboard wearing a unicorn costume, go for it (do some training first), or learn to play chopsticks on the piano but only with your toes, who am I to say no? BE random, be weird, but be specific in your weirdness.

7. MUST HAVE A SUCCESS-MARKER

"Starting something can be easy,
it is finishing it that is the highest hurdle."
Isabella Poretsis

When will you know you've ticked something off your Bucket List? When will you know you are successful? Just like there is a definite need for specificity in your Bucket List, so too is there a need for a success-marker. What is a success- marker? It's the end-step — the point you can say to yourself: 'Done' and tick it off the list. Most people when writing their first Bucket Lists (without my help) set standards rather than success-markers. The difference is that a success-marker is a definitive point, a standard sets a level that can be reached but also equally it's something you can fall back below as time goes on, so it never really ends. For example, 'To be photographed in Bali in my size 10 bikinis' is an end-step — the success-marker, while just 'Lose 15kg' is a standard. To you it might seem like it means the same thing, perhaps you feel like you need to lose 15kg before being seen in that bright pink two-piece on Kuta Beach, but it doesn't. 'Lose 15kg' is something you may feel you need to do again after you get back, so you have to take it off your

Reverse Bucket List and put it back on your Future Bucket List. No thanks. Set a Success Marker, that way you can tick it off and play on.

8. COPY, CHEAT AND STEAL

"If you steal from one author it's plagiarism;
if you steal from many it's research."
Wilson Mizner

In my seminars and keynote presentations I'm forever saying that you're allowed to do three things that you were told not to do in school:

1. You're allowed to copy.
2. You're allowed to cheat.
3. You're allowed to steal.

This is all in relation to Bucket List ideas of course!

I, like many, from a very early age have had instilled, almost ingrained in me, to never copy, cheat or steal — be it off fellow classmates, teammates, or from work colleagues. We are taught that we all must think for ourselves, to work independently, some may even attest to having their dreams suppressed to fit into the scarcity mindset (as opposed to the abundance mindset) of our general society.

I love to really encourage all of my fellow Bucket Listers to do the complete opposite of this when it comes to following The M.Y.B.U.C.K.E.T.L.I.S.T. Blueprint™. I strongly encourage all who are reading this book, all who hear me speak from stage to never judge what anyone else has written down on their Bucket List. In fact, during my keynote presentation I always say that there shall be no judgement in the room, no matter how different, quirky or downright bizarre some ideas may sound to you. More often than not I have found myself thinking, 'Damn, I really love that idea!', and consequently I have added this onto my very own Bucket List. When you hear an idea that sparks your interest, write it down.

It may not necessarily be under the same acronym you wish to place it, but that doesn't matter. Put it where it fits for you, as it must be truly personal.

Writing down all the things you wish to touch, feel, taste, or experience before your time is up should be the most personal and holistic Bucket List for you, things that really resonate with you. We've all heard for many years that if you steal, copy or cheat off someone that this is incorrect, immoral, even plagiarism. I personally believe that when you outsource, copy and, yes, even steal ideas from not just one source, but from many sources it should really be looked at as 'resourceful brilliance'. As humans, we naturally mimic those who we admire, those who inspire, and those who really hit our internal values, beliefs, core and vision.

9. NO JUDGEMENT

"The reason we struggle with insecurity is
because we compare our behind-the-scenes
with everyone else's highlights reel."
Steve Furtick

Unfortunately, a lot of people don't intimately share, let alone publicly declare what their goals are in life. Most lead a life of quiet desperation, hoping things will just 'turn out right'. Involving others in your goals is a key component of goal setting and goal achievement.

I've heard some weird stuff in my time speaking about Bucket Lists. As part of my talks, I have all attendees repeat after me 'It's ok to copy, cheat and steal and there's also to be no judgement!' I go on to say that, 'When you partner-up with the person next to you and they say that they want to do something a little freaky, or they have done something a little freaky, your response is to simply nod your head and say, 'Um...ok' and smile.' In all seriousness, who cares?

Stop caring about what other people think so much and do what you want. I think I speak on behalf of all the forty pluses out there when I say, 'the older you get, the less of a fuck you give'. Once you stop trying to impress everyone else you start to do more of what makes you happy. Over time we strengthen the 'I don't give a fuck muscle'. Believe me, the quicker you develop this muscle, the happier you'll be.

10. DON'T COMPARE OR COMPETE

"Comparison is the death of joy."
Mark Twain

Competition can kill you. Not only that, competition and comparison of Bucket Lists can kill your motivation to tick off your Bucket List items, and reduce the joy that they can bring you. If you are always comparing your achievements against other people's, you'll never feel the fulfilment and satisfaction you deserve when you do tick something on your list off. The 'mine is bigger than yours' macho bullshit won't fly here.

11. ONLY CLAIM IF WRITTEN

"Great goals make great people.
People cannot hit what they do not aim for."
Roy T. Bennett

This is important. You can't just claim something when you're there or if you happen to stumble across something you want to tick. You need to have it written down for it to count. You can still be pleased if you've done it, but if it wasn't intentional, it takes away from the intention driven Bucket List philosophy. What you can do though, is use that experience to come up with other Bucket List items. I'd like to say that this is officially a Bucket List Side Benefit.

12. BE PRESENT ON THE JOURNEY

"I made up my mind not to care so much about the
destination, and simply enjoy the journey."
David Archuleta

Beating yourself up because you didn't get to achieve that final end-step destination or (in other words) that Bucket List tick, is crazy. Having a Bucket List, becoming a Bucket Lister is more about who you develop into while accomplishing these things and less about the actual experiences, so if you don't get to the end-point on first or second or 32nd attempt, that's ok. You'll have grown so much by that point, it won't even matter. I want you to really pay attention to the growth of who you become on the journey towards your self-imposed destinations.

13. BE FLEXIBLE

"Flexibility is the greatest strength."
Steven Redhead

Things move. Goals shift. Perspectives vary. As your life's journey plays out, your attention to the things that light you up will change. This is a given. Just don't be too hard on yourself. All goals require flexibility.

There are quite a few Bucket List items that have been removed from my Bucket List over the years. There's also quite a few that are about to be dropped from my list. What you see in this book is what it is right for me now, at the time of writing these words. By the time it's published I can guarantee there'll be some things in here that I won't be into anymore. Being the goal-driven Taurean that I am, I have to let that go. Remember, this is truly about the journey, not the destination.

M: MEET A PERSONAL HERO

"IF YOU CAN TELL ME WHO YOUR HEROES ARE,
I CAN TELL YOU HOW YOU'RE GOING TO TURN OUT.
IT'S REALLY IMPORTANT TO HAVE THE RIGHT HEROES."
— WARREN BUFFETT —

Who are you paying attention to and why?

Who are your role models?

Who's a rock star or leader in your world?

Who are you a fanboy or fangirl of?

Who are you following on social media?

Who would you love to get a selfie with?

MEET A PERSONAL HERO
TRAV BELL

WHAT was your Bucket List item?
Meet Tim Ferriss.

WHY did you want to tick it off?
Tim shot to fame in 2007 after he published his book, *The 4 Hour Work Week*. Like a lot of his readers, I was blown away by his ideas around 'Lifestyle Design'. At the time of reading, I was transitioning out of my traditional 'bricks and mortar' personal fitness training studio businesses to do more speaking. The online world fascinated me because it appealed to one of my highest values...freedom. Instantly, he became the 'Yoda' of working online, life hacking, location independence, outsourcing, monetising your passions and living the digital nomad life. Of course, I had to meet the guru.

HOW did you tick it off?

Once 'Meeting Tim Ferris' landed on my Bucket List radar, I subscribed to his websites, stalked (or should I say) followed him on social media and paid close attention to his Australian event promoters. Not long after, he was due to do a gig in Melbourne. It was a breakfast presentation with a limited number of tickets for sale. My friend Rob and I committed straight away. The tickets weren't cheap, and it didn't guarantee a one-on-one catch-up, let alone a 'selfie'!

Tim spoke about his journey, the latest in tech, his daily rituals and routines, best hacks for life and business and he was also promoting his new book, *The 4 Hour Body*. In typical seminar form, the promoters offered us all something that Rob and I couldn't refuse. Offer #1 was to join Tim for a private Q and A, get a signed book and get a professional photo with Tim in another room. Offer #2 was do join the Q and A, get a signed book and the photo and also join Tim for lunch. That was only open to 20 people. About 25% of the 350 strong room went for Offer #1. While Rob and I joined the other 18 for the exclusive lunch as part of Offer #2. Did I have to pay to play? Big time! Offer #2 was $1,600 (from memory). Parting with $2K ($400 + $1600) to meet a personal hero was the hardest part of this journey for sure.

Ticking this Bucket List off was extremely impactful because I even got to sit next to Tim at lunch. Not without a bit of hustle either! When I bought the ticket to the lunch, I simply asked our host if I could sit next to him. I don't know if anyone else asked. But I did. So, she arranged it. If you don't ask, you don't get, right?

Of course, we talked Bucket Lists. And I'm pleased to say he's not arrogant! He's a cool guy. This experience has taught me that it's ok to pay to play if it means enough to you. Everyone is accessible.

MEET A PERSONAL HERO
JIM SKIVALIDAS

WHAT was your Bucket List item?
Meet Paul Stanley from KISS.

WHY did you want to tick it off?
A few years ago, I lost my Chiropractic clinic to a fire. With all my personal belongings gone it was a huge financial hit. I started to question my life's decisions. In 2011 I took up singing lessons. But never gathered the courage to do anything live. Let alone in a band. It was a real interest of mine. It inspired me. But I didn't have the guts to go for it.

HOW did you tick it off?
I didn't have this on my Bucket List long before ticking it off. Within 6 weeks I sang for the first time in a band. May 2016

in Richmond, Australia. I was addicted to being the 'front man' after that. Admiring other 'front men', I found that Paul Stanley and Don Felder (who wrote Hotel California, from the Eagles) were performing in LA and running a 'Rock Program' too. I loved KISS. I had to meet Paul Stanley! The first step to ticking this off was booking it. I couldn't turn back then.

It was $5,000 plus return flights and accommodation in the US. I literally flew out on a Wednesday from Australia, yet I arrived on their Wednesday. Started training and learning songs on the Thursday and Friday and then performed Saturday and Sunday night. It was crazy! This all took place at the Whiskey Go Go Bar in Los Angeles. Famous for bands like the Doors and Motley Crue.

I met Paul Stanley from KISS. It was late June 2016. I even had the blessing of singing his signature song, 'Love Gun' while he played rhythm guitar! Inspirational, to say the least. And yes, I was dressed in 'my own unique' makeup and theatrical clothing too.

Ticking this off was incredible. I believe in having a Bucket List. It's fuel to inspire you to do more of the things you love. Not for money, but to do something that turns on your juices of life!

I'm now in 2 bands, recording weekly and getting great practice. This also laid a great public speaking foundation for me. Between being a chiropractor, family life, music and public speaking, it's a balancing act. But it's worth it.

50 IDEAS TO MEET A PERSONAL HERO

- A favourite sports star
- A favourite movie star
- Childhood hero
- A champion of a cause
- A long-lost relative
- The head of a charity
- A radio personality
- An adventurer
- An inventor
- Favourite news presenter
- Favourite comedian
- Favourite reality TV star
- An inspiring author
- An inspiring coach e.g.: sports, life or business
- Your favourite actress/actor
- A great role-model
- Another person who has overcome a tragedy
- Another Bucket Lister
- A medal winner
- Head of the defence force
- A war hero
- Favourite singer
- Your favourite band
- Talk show host
- A politician
- A religious leader
- A group of heroes e.g.: lifeguards, firefighters
- Cancer survivor
- Sports team

SIR RICHARD BRANSON

- Your biological parents
- An influential teacher
- Women's rights champion
- A favourite animal activist
- A famous surgeon
- An entrepreneur superhero
- State Governor/Premier
- Leader of your preferred political party
- Someone prominent you disagree with
- A past President
- The leader of your country
- A movie director
- A Summer Olympic gold medal winner
- A Winter Olympic gold medal winner
- Someone you've modelled yourself on
- Emmy, Grammy, Oscar, Tony Award Winner
- Nobel Peace Prize Winner
- A favourite cartoon or comic creator
- Someone from another country

GARY VEE

CADEL EVANS

YOUR TURN

My Meet A Personal Hero will be:

TIP

1. Start small — subscribe to their stuff
and read their books.

2. Offer to be an intern — they are busy, they like
people who have the time that they don't have.

3. Pay to play — if they run programs or events
pay the price to attend.

Y: YOUR PROUD ACHIEVEMENTS

"I HOPE YOU LIVE A LIFE YOU'RE PROUD OF. IF YOU FIND
YOU'RE NOT, I HOPE YOU HAVE THE STRENGTH
TO START ALL OVER AGAIN."
— F. SCOTT FITZGERALD —

What do you want to be really proud of before your time is up?

What do you want to look back on during the span of your life?

*What will give you a sense of achievement, fulfilment or
satisfaction when you complete it?*

What are your success benchmarks?

*When will you know you're successful in your
personal and professional life?*

What have you always wanted to achieve?

YOUR PROUD ACHIEVEMENTS
TRAV BELL

WHAT was the item on your Bucket List?
Do a TED Talk.

WHY did you want to tick this off?
The thought leadership shared through TED Talks has always inspired me. People chosen to speak on a TED stage are normally at the forefront of their respective fields. For me, a TED or TEDx talk validated ideas worth spreading...as their motto suggests. Do I have an idea in me that is worth spreading? Can I add value to people? Can I get people to look at a certain part of their life differently? Can I change the conversation? Can I have an impact? Can I leave a legacy through my ideas? It's one thing being recognised as a Professional Speaker (which is what I am today), but it's another being recognised as a real Thought Leader on a topic.

HOW did you tick it off?

To make my goal more specific, I focused my attention on TEDx Melbourne. The biggest in Australia. Therefore, I had to find out who was responsible for running this event. That was the connection I needed. Not to mention getting on their radar to be considered for a slot.

As a member of Professional Speakers Australia (PSA) and ex-State president for PSA in Victoria, Australia, I knew Jon Yeo, the curator and Licence holder for TEDx Melbourne was a member of PSA too. So about 18 months before I ended up getting on stage at TEDx Melbourne, I invited Jon on my Bucket List Life podcast where I spent most of the podcast asking the most obvious questions about speaking on a TEDx stage. Every question angled towards that. Sucking-up did no good. Jon didn't take the bait. Just applying wasn't any better. I left it alone and got busy doing my keynote speeches and seminars. By doing that, people started seeing me more and more.

About 6 months out from TEDx, I ran into Jon at another Speakers' dinner, and just said Hi. Then, as he was leaving he said 'Trav, we should have a conversation about you doing a TED talk.' I lost my shit right there, I managed to keep it cool on the outside, but I was doing little fist pumps on the inside. I still had to 'audition'. This was the moment to shine in front of Jon. So, I presented my idea, got to the end of it, and Jon, said, 'Do you normally talk about this stuff?'. I tentatively said, 'yeah'. Then he said something, I'll never forget. He said, 'Great! Don't change a thing!'. I was speechless.

I did a few tweaks in the lead-up. 'No canned keynotes. Not too polished. It's all about the idea worth spreading,' he said. In front of 2000 people, 4 cameras, on a 3 X 3 red dot, I ticked 'Do A TED Talk' off my Bucket List, live. It was an amazing experience.

YOUR PROUD ACHIEVEMENTS
OLLIE GLADWELL

WHAT was the item on your Bucket List?
Get married and walk on a beach together.

WHY did you want to tick this off?
My gorgeous husband and I had been separated from when we were 14 after my family moved from the UK to Australia. We were inseparable when we were at high school up until nearly 15. He was my everything. However, my life in the UK was not at all as it seemed on the surface so whilst we were close he had no idea of what secrets I held in my head. We walked home from school every day but could not do 'normal' things such as go to the movies, go down to the river and just be together outside of school. I dreamed of these things. My now husband had no idea of my life that was going on within my family. So, we moved — with me knowing we would not see each other again — he was gorgeous, and I knew he would not wait for me. Nor could he — in those days there was no internet or Skype.

Fast forward 37 years and through the magic of the internet we connected, and I went to the UK. The minute we met up again we knew nothing had changed. The feelings were just the same. So here we were from different parts of the world but with a beautiful Aunt in the UK who told us we had to make it happen. And he did. He left his business, his life and came to Australia to be with me in September 2012. I was part of the Melton Chamber of Commerce and we attended a networking night where Trav spoke. We both had realised early on we had missed so many things — even when we were young, and we needed to fast track everything as we only had limited summers left. We knew based on 'summers' we had to do as many firsts as possible. Simple things were as important as the big-ticket items. We came back from that night and made our lists. Most of them related to travel but there were plenty of 'normal' things — going to the movies and walking together on a deserted beach were two of mine.

HOW did you tick it off?

We created a Bucket List the night we heard Trav talk at a Melton dinner. My now husband Paul had only been here two weeks from the UK; we came straight home and made our lists and have been working on them ever since.

The biggest thing we needed was time and opportunity. We had about eight weeks to plan and carry out a wedding, get all the paperwork to immigration and prove to them that we were fair dinkum about being together. In between we were trying to keep ourselves afloat with Paul not being able to work. We managed to tick off going to the movies, in 'Gold Class' no less! However, we could not see in between working and getting Paul to meet people, that the walk on the beach would get ticked off. There was going to be no honeymoon. We couldn't afford it. However, my amazing workmates and the two wonderful directors of the company I worked for all chipped in to give us a weekend away on the Mornington Peninsula — including dinner. I had now gotten myself closer to the beach — the rest was about timing!

We arrived in Mornington and had a wonderful, amazing and incredible stay in the most beautiful homestead. We had dinner overlooking the sea and realised this was not the time. There were people everywhere! We decided that the next morning would be ideal — we would find the beach when everyone was at work! So off we went to find it. Eventually we found a beach with not a soul on it — I was so excited that I ran down the stairs to get to the beach. I always remember looking back at Paul as he walked down the beach towards me — head into the wind but a huge smile on his face. He picked me up and twirled me around — it was perfect. We walked the length of the beach arm in arm and I then drew a heart in the sand with our initials in it — very corny but I am sure at 14 I would have done this too!

I think for me this one experience was so important. We lived by the sea when we were kids and we never got to walk by it together. I had thought about it heaps when we were young, but it never happened due to some challenges I faced everyday within my family. This day — even though it was windy, was perfect, everything I thought it would be — the boy who made me feel safe at 14 when he hugged me was with me on a deserted beach with his big arms around me making me feel safe. It was the most incredible feeling. Like coming home.

BECOME A
CERTIFIED
SPEAKING
PROFESSIONAL
(CSP)

50 IDEAS OF YOUR PROUD ACHIEVEMENTS

- Start a business
- Live comfortably off passive income
- Sell a business
- Dunk a basketball
- Hit a home run
- Graduate from University/ College
- Get a Diploma
- Complete an MBA
- Complete a PHD
- Crack a whip
- Create an app
- Win a community award
- Win a business award
- Win a Nobel Prize
- Go international with your business
- Get married
- Become a citizen of another country
- Become a foster parent
- Become a parent
- Achieve a Black Belt in Karate
- Sponsor a child
- First house
- Travel overseas
- Learn your partner's first language

- Land an acting role in a movie
- Get your car, boat, motorcycle or truck license
- Create a support program
- Represent your country in sport
- Retire your parents
- Find a cure for a disease
- Make your house run on Green Energy
- Adopt a child
- Rehabilitate yourself
- Become a pet volunteer
- Touch your first pregnant belly
- Build a School

- Coach a team to a grand final
- Put a stop to puppy farms
- Write a gratitude list for 365 days
- Publish your own book
- Fill your own event
- Star in your own TV show
- Become a Celebrant
- Race a car you built
- Be debt-free
- Give a motivational speech at a High School
- Build a Hospital
- Raise a Family
- TED Talk
- First car

YOUR TURN

My Your Proud Achievement will be:

TIP

1. Visualise yourself on your deathbed (morbid, I know) ...what does a regretful life feel like in comparison to a regret-free life?

2. Relook at those 80 squares again!

3. Step into your 'future self' having already achieved your goal. What do you see, hear, feel? What are people saying about you? How do you feel within yourself now?

B: BUY THAT SPECIAL SOMETHING

"YOU GET TO A CERTAIN AGE, AND YOU FEEL
THE NEED TO REWARD YOURSELF JUST
FOR EXISTING."
— RUFUS WAINWRIGHT —

What do you want to buy for yourself?

What would you like to buy for someone else?

How would you like to reward yourself in the short-term?

How would you like to reward yourself in the long-term?

What's that one thing you've always wanted?

What's something that would really motivate you to work towards?

BUY THAT SPECIAL SOMETHING
TRAV BELL

WHAT was the item on your Bucket List?
Get a tailored suit made.

WHY did you want to tick it off?

As a speaker, I often get invited to attend gala dinners, awards nights and so on, and for everyone I was having to hire Tuxedos. They never fit very well, they didn't look awesome and they weren't very 'me'.

I'm a bit of a minimalist so buying stuff for myself is usually a pretty low priority, but I also know that it's important to reward myself and celebrate the victories I have in life. Rewarding myself for getting to speak at this conference with a tailored 'Trav Bell' suit, meant that I could tick off a Bucket List item at the same time, that was pretty compelling.

HOW did you tick it off?

I ticked this item off in May 2014 in Singapore. I was there to speak at the Asian Public Speakers Association annual conference.

I landed in Singapore and got straight to shopping. I'd already asked a fellow speaker from Australia where to get it made because he'd already had some done himself. With that info I headed to the area my mate had recommended and started shopping around. A lot of them seemed a bit sketchy but I finally found one I liked, got measured up, chose all the details, including fabric, lapels, even T.B. monogramming on the cuffs and: 'The Bucket List Guy' stitched into the inside of the jacket. Once that was done, it only took them 24 hours to have it ready to go and $700 down, I walked away looking awesome in a suit that really suited me!

Highs of the experience included the look and feel of the suit once it was on and I had it. The lows were basically trying to work out which one of the huge number of tailors was going to do a great job and not charge me huge amounts of money, for a crap job.

The experience of ticking this off the list was excellent, I looked great and got heaps of comments on it at the Gala Dinner I needed it for. I continue to wear it regularly, so I've gotten plenty of value out of it, it's also different than most suits so it's a conversation starter and I've been able to use the story of buying it in my talks, so it has bought heaps of excellent value.

I often talk about the ripple effect of ticking a Bucket List item off. For me I have added two more to my list. I'm going to get a couple more suits done next time I'm in Singapore. I've also added a Hublot Watch to my Bucket List since then.

BUY THAT SPECIAL SOMETHING
KEN ZELAZNY

WHAT was the item on your Bucket List?
Buy a Rolex watch for each of my 3 sons.

WHY did you want to tick it off?
Back in 2011 when I wrote my Bucket List, Brad Sugars took us through this exercise of 101 things to do before you die. I think at about 65 on this list I put, when I become a Millionaire and have one million dollars in the bank I would buy my 3 boys Christopher, Trevor and Kyle a Rolex watch.

In April 2017, on that fatal day, I went to a doctor's appointment where they found a mass on my right kidney. They told me I had cancer. I was told that I had to have my right kidney removed as it was cancerous. It weighed 2½ lbs when it was only supposed to weigh .2lbs. To be completely honest, it scared the shit out of me. The first thing that went through my mind on that day in April was, I've got to start ticking off Bucket List items because I just don't know where this is going.

HOW did you tick it off?

At that time, I called a really good friend of mine who owns a high-end jewellery store and sells Rolex Tag and all the other big boys. I said, 'Hey, I want 3 watches pronto, I want the deluxe and I want them inscribed, *'Love Dad, December 5th 1962, Perseverance'*. My birthday, and perseverance a word I continually push towards my boys was inscribed on the back of all 3 watches.

I then immediately flew my son, his fiancé and my Grand Puppy (grandfather) home from the West Coast and gathered my other 2 sons who already lived close by. We all then gathered together on May 10th, 2017, 2 weeks prior to my operation. They were all confused and didn't know what to expect. I told them the news that I had Cancer. Initially they were shocked, I then brought out the watches, which shocked them even more! They couldn't believe I was doing what I was doing. They appreciated it and haven't taken them off since that day.

The cancer was a wake-up effect for a lot of people, to pay it forwards. It has made me just a little more philanthropic, wherever I can. As recently as just yesterday I stopped in at a restaurant. There was a guy standing there at the counter saying; 'I can only spend seven dollars and thirty cents on my lunch'. I insisted he take $20 and go eat. The guy wouldn't take it, and then everybody in the restaurant started saying; 'Hey take it! It's a generous offer, he's trying to be nice!'. I got support from the crowd, that was just so encouraging too. I guess it's just as simple as giving back to people who aren't as fortunate as others. In whatever capacity I can help; I will help.

50 IDEAS TO BUY THAT SPECIAL SOMETHING

- A gold Rolex
- A beach house
- A collector's item
- A rare piece of art
- A Segway
- A Tesla
- A Wally yacht
- A diamond ring
- A personalised suit
- A 1st class flight
- An amazing ball gown
- Matching diamond jewellery

- Flying lessons
- Scuba diving lessons
- The services of an in-house cleaner/chef
- An around-the-world ticket
- A dream piece of land
- Designer furniture
- Hot air balloon ride over Cappadocia, Turkey
- A tiara
- A horse
- A dog
- A 1st class around-the-world ticket
- A helicopter ride
- A cruise

BUY A PERSONALISED MONEY CLIP

BUY A BEACH HOUSE

- An antique musical instrument
- A Ferrari
- A full day of pampering
- A private lesson or coaching session
- A personal development seminar
- Italian leather boots
- Designer handbag
- Designer sunglasses
- A holiday for your parents
- A new computer
- A year's subscription to your favourite mag
- An outdoor adventure
- An in-ground pool
- A glamour photo shoot

- Tickets to your most favourite performer's concert
- A 4-post king-size bed
- Build and fill your dream library
- A house boat
- Tickets to the Ellen DeGeneres Show
- An investment property
- A car for your parents
- A pontoon boat
- A bike
- A drone
- An acre of land on the moon

YOUR TURN

My Buy That Special Something will be:

TIP

1. Start very, very small. Reward yourself today, it will create a Bucket List snowball effect.

2. Remember to buy yourself a birthday present to celebrate another year on earth —go ahead, you deserve it!

3. Buy something for someone else today - again, start small and build the 'Thank You Muscle'.

V: ULTIMATE CHALLENGES

"THE ULTIMATE MEASURE OF A MAN IS NOT WHERE HE STANDS IN MOMENTS OF COMFORT AND CONVENIENCE, BUT WHERE HE STANDS AT TIMES OF CHALLENGE AND CONTROVERSY."
— MARTIN LUTHER KING JR. —

What are the small physical challenges you'd like to complete?

What are the medium physical challenges you'd like to accomplish?

What are the big physical challenges you'd like to achieve?

What events around the world would you like to compete in?

What would really push your comfort zone?

What's something out of character that you are curious about?

ULTIMATE CHALLENGES
TRAV BELL

WHAT was the item on your Bucket List?
Follow the Tour De France...on a bike.

WHY did you want to tick it off?
Being a cyclist, I've always been a huge fan of the Tour and watched it. I'm so inspired by it and the athletes. The whole tour goes through such beautiful scenery, the old towns, the whole of France is just really cool, so I've always imagined myself doing it. Little did I know I'd have to climb some hills in the process.

HOW did you tick it off?
This had been a long-term item on my Bucket List, for about 5 years. I ticked it off July 2017 in the southern French Alps and in Paris.

It's funny, once you write it down, it becomes real. I'd told some people that I wanted to do it, and talked about it, I just didn't know when I'd be able to put it together. I do some charity rides with some guys I used to ride with when I was living in Melbourne, there's a core group of about 10 of us, and it just came up in conversation that we all wanted to go over and give it a crack. Low and behold, we made it happen.

Where I live, on the Australian South Coast, it's very flat. When I ride, on average I only do about 150 to 200 meters elevation, whereas over there, it's significantly different. Running a business, doing all the other things I have to do on a daily basis and finding time to train for the kind of steep ascents that the French Alps have was quite difficult.

The hardest thing was training in winter for the European summer and staying consistent with that training. Then finding hills whenever I could. Once we received the elevation profile of what we'd be doing; up for 2km, then down for 2km then up for another 2km, it looked like a sound wave. That's when I knew I had to get serious about it, that's when I realised this really was going to be an Ultimate Challenge, and that I wasn't going to be able to half-arse it. So, I went out, got myself a new, lighter bike, a new kit and really knuckled down.

The first day, when we arrived in Grenoble in the south of France, we got our hire bikes and went out. We were supposed to be doing a 'warm up ride', then the next thing you know we're doing 8.5% inclines climbing 1500 meters, in the middle of the day, in 33 °C heat. I realised then that we were in for one hell of a journey here. We then followed the final week of the Tour de France, which runs for three weeks, the last week is when they are in the Alps.

Some of the highs include doing famous climbs like L'Alpe Du Huez, which has twenty-one hair pin turns, Col du Telegraphe and Col du Galibier. Seeing all of these beautiful sights and getting heaps of photos and videos was so memorable. We got to see the start of a stage, with the cameras, helicopters and the whole circus. We got to see the finish of a stage, where an Australian, Michael Matthews, won the sprinters' jersey that day. Getting to see the riders come through a mountain pass was incredible too. We'd done that ride in the morning and we were all on our lowest gear to get up it, then these guys came through on their large chain ring (a much harder gear for the non-cyclists out there) just grinding it out, trying to break through. It was next level to see.

We really got to experience the vibe of the Tour and got to tick off some of those big Bucket List climbs and the big descents, that makes riding in the French Alps so memorable. But also, when you are doing these climbs you do ask yourself the big questions, 'Why the fuck am I doing this?' 'Why did I sign up for this?'. You really are at your threshold of capacity. Your heart rate is through the roof, you're going through all the water, going through all the supplements, trying not to stop, knowing fair well you've got to keep soldiering on. Heck, there are times you want to throw your bike off the side of the mountain. Then you get to the top and start coming down the other side; now you feel like superman, you feel unstoppable. So, cycling, particularly on this trip, was really emotional.

We actually got to ride down the finishing chute on one of the stages, as the last public riders to come down before the pros came through. There were people lining the sides of the road, all cheering and chanting 'Allez, Allez, Allez' which is 'Go, Go, Go'. Coming down the chute with a tail wind, after we'd just flogged ourselves doing that stage, that's a moment I'll never forget. It's in those moments, the pain goes away really quickly and where you realise every little bit of the journey was worth it.

ULTIMATE CHALLENGES
TRAVIS BECKLEY

WHAT was the item on your Bucket List?
Complete an Ironman triathlon.

WHY did you want to tick it off?
I had a mate, Brad, that was into this sport. He did it regularly and fairly easily as he is a good athlete, for me it was going to be a lot harder and more of a life achievement.

HOW did you tick it off?
I ticked this off in Port Macquarie in May of 2012 after only putting this item on my list 12 months prior. I guess this is a relatively short time to tick off a Bucket List item.

Entering the race was the first step to committing. At $900 registration, it was a significant first step, also. Overall this Ironman cost me about $10, 000. It all added up in the end: Buying a bike, runners, clothing, helmets, shoes, accommodation, race entry, nutrition, flights etc. I also started to connect with other like-minded people that were prioritising their health and fitness.

Along the way, the training progressively got harder. Although I was getting fitter the program continued to push me out of my comfort zone into areas I had never been physically. Mentally it started to become fatiguing also as the magnitude of the event started to consume my every thought. I went through periods throughout the training where I thought I would make the finish line easily and then during other training sets, I would fear I was nowhere near the standard required.

There were several training sets where I walked away feeling defeated. But looking back, in hindsight now, I know those particular sessions made me stronger, so these days I embrace them.

Starting race morning before the gun went off for the swim, I felt like I had already ticked 'Do an Ironman' off my Bucket List. Although I hadn't yet raced yet, even making the start line, healthy and fit was a real achievement. During the race, like in training, I had highs and lows as my mind and body fought between the pain and desire to finish. Running down the finishers chute in Port Macquarie with thousands of people cheering, including my wife, was a moment I will never forget. It was an addictive feeling that has since seen me go back to do more Ironman races.

I have now put other Ironman races around the world on my list. I see it as a great way to complete a physical challenge and also travel Australia and the world. I have also put other Ultimate Challenges on my Bucket List that I previously thought would be out of my capability. Such as the 3 Peaks Bike Ride in Victoria, an overseas marathon, an

Ultra Marathon, Mt Kilimanjaro and more!

Completing this Ironman (or even just putting it on my list) has positively affected my life in terms of health, mental attitude, attitudes to fear, and what I am capable of. The ripple effect is now my friends have been inspired to join me on this journey and together we regularly train for races around Australia. When I am training I am happy, mentally alert and it draws the best out of me. It has taught me that, 'anything is possible'.

WALK THE KOKODA TRACK WITH DAD

CLIMB MT KILIMANJARO

50 IDEAS FOR ULTIMATE CHALLENGES

- Complete a 1/2 or full marathon
- Bench press my own body weight
- Complete in a triathlon
- Compete in a bodybuilding/ figure competition
- Compete in Tough Mudder
- Compete in a Spartan Race
- Complete the Kokoda Track
- Compete in a boxing match
- Summit Mt Everest
- Complete the 7 summits
- Complete an Ironman
- Climb Mt Kilimanjaro
- Complete a 5km or 10km run
- Change occupations
- Represent your state in your sport
- Leave an abusive spouse
- Starting IVF treatment to become a parent
- Represent your country at the Olympics
- Swim the English Channel
- Compete in the CrossFit games
- Go to the South and/or North Pole
- Complete an adventure race
- Learn to juggle
- Move to another country and learn the language
- Climb an active volcano
- Come out to family and friends
- Live off the land for a week
- Hit a hole in one
- Walk on a high wire
- Shoot par on your favourite golf course
- Compete in the Tour Down Under, Australia
- Cycle 1000km in a week
- 7+ day fast

THIS IS YOU REACHING THE SUMMIT OF MT EVEREST

CYCLE THROUGH THE HIMALAYAS

COMPLETE A HALF MARATHON

- Visit all 50 States in the USA
- Visit a silent retreat
- Set a World Record
- Catch and release a Blue Marlin
- Compete in an international sports event
- Singapore to Shanghai on a motorbike
- Run a 4-minute mile
- Run for a seat in Government
- Trek the Great Rift Valley in Kenya
- Kayak the length of the Nile River, Africa
- Complete a paddle race
- Video blog for 365 days in a row
- Read 52 books in a year
- 50 push ups a day for a year
- Reach a major milestone in entertainment
- Create a passive income business
- Get barrelled on a surfboard

YOUR TURN

My Ultimate Challenge will be:

TIP

1. Mix your Ultimate Challenge list up with mental, intellectual and physical challenges.

2. Start something today that challenges you e.g., going live on social media for 7 days— that may lead to 365 days, that may lead to a YouTube channel, book or blog.

3. Focus on and get excited about the bigger version of you that is waiting on the other side of your challenges.

(: CONQUER A FEAR

"EVERYTHING YOU WANT IS ON THE
OTHER SIDE OF FEAR."
— **JACK CANFIELD** —

What have you always been afraid of?

*What's a fear (if overcome) that would help you in your
business, career or relationships?*

What's something that has made you very uncomfortable?

*What's a fear (if overcome) that excites you about what's
on the other side?*

What's a fear that has been holding you back?

What's a fear you've been scared to admit to yourself?

CONQUER A FEAR
TRAV BELL

WHAT was the item on your Bucket List?
Nude model for a life drawing class.

WHY did you want to tick it off?
Still to this day, I don't know why I did this one or why I even put it on my Bucket List to begin with. I suppose I put it on my list really just to expand my experience. I wasn't comfortable with it, and I don't like being uncomfortable with stuff, so I put it down. It's the same reason I put bungie jumping and the other things on my Conquer a Fear section of my list. The vulnerability, that exposure, is something I'm always pushing. If there is a part of me that says, 'Nah, don't' I will do it, just to counteract it. Plus, I always knew it would make a great story.

HOW did you tick it off?

I ticked this off in Seddon (West of Melbourne) in 2012 after it being on my Bucket List for about 6 months.

I wasn't overly motivated to tick this off. I put it down on the list. Then I saw a sign at the art studio, and if I hadn't been given a prompt from someone saying, 'You won't do that', it might still be waiting to be ticked off.

Walking into the shop front, with all the curtains pulled down, in the middle of winter, was frankly terrifying. The owner of art studio just casually said, 'You'll be laying here' gesturing to some red velvet chairs, for me to lounge on. She said, 'Get changed over there, people will be arriving soon'. I took off my clothes and put a robe on, and then thought, 'What am I doing?'. I asked the owner how she wanted me to sit and she said, 'Just sit or stand however you like and we'll instruct you how we'd like you to be depending on the lighting and what the students want to see. From memory between 10 and 15 people were there, all behind these big artists easels. I walked out into the middle of the circle of artists and over to the chair, just about to disrobe, when another girl walked in. I was thinking, 'Ok, who's this?' thinking she was part of the art class, I was wrong, she just started stripping off right there. I was thinking, 'What the fuck?!' I didn't realise I was going to be modelling with another person, particularly not a very attractive young woman! She came over and I just tried not to look at her, and we just took instruction from there, in different poses and positions. Now, as you know by now, I've studied a lot of psychology, done a lot of mindset and personal development over the years, but I have to admit, I had to channel all of that to 'talk it down' if you know what I mean!

The experience was overall a good one. The owner of the studio did a piece of me for me, it was very abstract, which was really cool. The really awkward small talk with my co-model, is funny to look back on. Plus, I left with a huge sense of fulfilment, $50 in my hand and a really great story, that I've been able to use for years.

There is always a ripple effect. I know people who have put this on their Bucket Lists because of me doing it, and I have had quite a few women come up to me at seminars saying that they have lingerie/glamour shoots on their lists now too.

I learned to not hang around with people who will dare me to do stuff, because I'll just do it. Here is some advice for you if you do decide to copy this one. Avoid doing it in the small town where you live, buy coffee every day etc. Also, don't do it in winter and make sure you know whether you are doing it alone or with a co-model.

I've now added 'be part of a Spencer Tunick photo' to my Bucket List.

BUNGEE JUMPING

CONQUER A FEAR
TRACEY HICKMOTT

WHAT was the item on your Bucket List?
To overcome agoraphobia (a type of anxiety disorder).

WHY did you want to tick it off?
To live a free life away from the confines of the walls of my home. There were so many things I wanted to do and see; my children were growing up and I couldn't live a moment longer knowing that I wasn't living to my full potential. When I began to realise how restricting this disorder actually was for me, I knew something had to change. I was done being comfortable.

HOW did you tick it off?
For 10 years I had been seeing a psychiatrist every two weeks who kept me stable and sane during times of uncertainty. He was amazing and is one of the main reasons I am the parent I am proud to be today. My children were the biggest driver in overcoming my agoraphobia. They were growing up and older, I knew that something needed to change if I was going to bring them into the world and model to them a life I was truly passionate about. One of happiness and true freedom.

I learned to become present in the now and began to focus on goals and dreams for myself. I felt my horizons broadening and was ready to make real change.

I sought out the most intelligent people I could, which required a lot of courage and for me to let go of my ego... as anybody with a similar disorder would know the struggle of being so far away from who they know they are and who they know they can be.

I was too used to my therapist. I needed someone who would really challenge me. Through my years I had become a master of deception and was exceptional at falsely leading people to believe I was happy and okay. Now I was ready. I was more open to be challenged, more open to looking deeper.

I worked with this coach for 12 months. 12 months was all it took. It's funny the collapse in time that happens when you're actually seeking change, not just thinking about it.

My coach was intuitive, intelligent and strong. He couldn't be conned by any of the programs I had learned in the past. He simply saw through my bullshit and facade. But most importantly he saw my dedication and potential.

I am proud to say that after a lot of extremely hard and challenging moments which felt like lifetimes; I can now live life outside of my home panic-free. I have helped my children blossom by living an aligned life, and for the first time in my life I have travelled overseas (multiple times now) and to my dream destination, Italy.

I own and operate a commercial art business and I can say that I am truly happy with who I am and where I am in life. I am thrilled to see what else I can do. As now I have overcome this fear, I feel liberated.

50 IDEAS TO CONQUER A FEAR

- Fire-walk
- Busk
- Overcome a phobia
- Swim with Great White sharks
- Crocodile Cage of Death
- Tandem skydive
- Solo skydive
- Participate in a Spencer Tunick photo
- Publicly speak to a crowd of 100-1000 people
- Abseil
- Rap-Jump off a building
- Ski a black run
- Luge
- Fly in a plane
- Sail in a boat
- Go in a submarine
- Parasail
- Hang glide
- Play music in front of a crowd
- BASE jump
- Propose to the one you love
- Dance in public
- Do improv
- Walk on an observation deck
- Sing in front of a paying audience
- Move to another country
- Perform a stand-up comedy gig
- Walk a tightrope
- Swim in an open-water swim event
- Let a spider crawl on you
- Go caving
- Go on an internet, speed or blind date
- Go into a haunted house
- Write a book and have it published
- Go on the world's highest/longest zip-line
- Document your life on your YouTube channel
- Release an album of your own music
- Be a contestant on a TV show
- Bungee jump
- Do the George Swing at Victoria Falls
- Wrap a snake around you
- Drag race
- Ask for a raise
- Host a dinner party that you cooked
- Publicly debate
- Go on a TV talent show
- Camp alone in the woods
- Cliff dive
- Travel alone
- Go to a circus and talk to a clown

YOUR TURN

My Conquer A Fear will be:

TIP

1. REMEMBER - get excited about the bigger version of you that's waiting beyond the fear!

2. Do something that scares you every day - e.g. go and get rejected for something today and build your Rejection/Fear muscle.

3. When facing a fear, think about how the psychology of overcoming it can be replicated into other areas of your life.

K: KIND ACTS FOR OTHERS

"SERVICE TO OTHERS IS THE RENT YOU PAY
FOR YOUR ROOM HERE ON EARTH."
— MUHAMMAD ALI —

What's a cause that's close to your heart?

Have you or a loved one been affected by something?

What's something that you are passionate about getting behind?

*What saddens you or pisses you off that you could
do something about?*

*What would you like to give more money,
time and/or attention to?*

*How can you contribute in your community —
nationally or globally?*

KIND ACTS FOR OTHERS
TRAV BELL

WHAT was the item on your Bucket List?
Volunteer at an orphanage over Christmas.

WHY did you want to tick it off?
The fact that I had never done anything like this before. Every time Christmas comes around I honestly do think of other people, I don't really think of myself and I don't really want for much in terms of presents. It's a great time to connect and bring families together, which is why Christmas is so great.

Prior to doing this I've always wanted to volunteer over Christmas but never quite gotten around to doing it. As I was overseas for Christmas, I thought well I'm kind of at a loose end here and I didn't want to spend it by myself in Cambodia. So, what was I going to do?

HOW did you tick it off?

After traveling through Cambodia with a friend and seeing some amazing places, the journey was coming to an end. Knowing that my traveling partner had to go back to work after we got to Vietnam I was sort of at a loose end. I didn't want to go home, as I wanted to keep traveling. I also had this chip on my shoulder not knowing what I was going to do for Christmas. Then it all fell into place.

We were down at the river front in Phnom Penh, where we saw a young group of Australians wearing the same charity shirts all spruiking, 'New Hope for Cambodian Children'. We got talking and they told me they were going to an orphanage and spending a week helping build schools and teach English. This has always fascinated me. It was on the Bucket List to go and help at an orphanage, but I had no idea it was going to happen this way. I got the details and went from there.

The next day we followed the route and went to Vietnam, where I sent an email to the orphanage. They replied promptly saying they could use another set of hands to help pack the presents that had been donated for Christmas if I were to come back through Cambodia.

So, I followed through. I started as a teacher's aide for half a week and when they finished their school year it was basically straight into Christmas. I was staying in the dorm with all these school kids and teachers, eating food with them, getting to know them, it was truly a great experience. The next role for me was to hang out with the teachers and help pack the presents into Santa sacks. For a couple of days, we packed all these Santa sacks full of toys for the children at the school. There were 250 kids who were all orphans and were all HIV+. Many, unfortunately, didn't live that long.

When Christmas came around the founder of the orphanage dressed up as Santa and I was basically his body guard, as the kids would just jump all over Santa if no one was there to help. I dressed in an ill-fitting elf outfit and helped give out presents on that day. Seeing the reactions of the kids is something I will never forget. After this I helped out for another couple of days before continuing on traveling.

At that time, having never being involved or seeing an orphanage before or even how the whole system was run, made me very, very humbled. Being adopted myself and seeing these kids who don't have parents connect with you the way they did, made it extremely, extremely hard when I couldn't adopt every single one of them. This experience made me appreciate Christmas a little bit more and what the founders of these sorts of charities do, in giving up a big chunk of their life to help others. I think this item was the catalyst to make my Bucket List a lot less selfish and more selfless.

KIND ACTS
FOR OTHERS IS
ALSO HELPING
OTHERS TICK
OFF THEIR
BUCKET LIST

KIND ACTS FOR OTHERS
STACEY NICOLE NOWAK

WHAT *was the item on your Bucket List?*
Donate blood.

WHY *did you want to tick it off?*
I put donating blood on my Bucket List about 5 months ago for several reasons. Donating blood is such a 'simple' K – kind act for others, however for me it is much more than simple. Not only is it a 'K', it helped push me and grow me to C – conquer a fear as I hate needles. I was also very curious as to what my blood type is (S – satisfy a curiosity). It is so important to know your blood type in case someone you know, and love needs it or if you have a rare type. Donating one pint of blood can save up to 3 lives. The reason why I decided to tick this off when I did is I was having THE MOST DIFFICULT week of my life. I was finalizing my divorce — talk about conquering a fear. I figured I if I had to be brave enough to get up on the stand to finalize my divorce, donating blood should be a piece of cake. That same week why mother was admitted into the ICU as she had a heart condition that we didn't know about. People are in constant need of blood. Only 13% of the population ever donates blood in the United States but someone needs blood every 2 seconds.

As a Certified Bucket List Coach®, it is my job to make sure that I am practicing what I preach. Because it was such a difficult week I went straight to my Bucket List Board and thought to myself, when tough times hit, you better make sure that you are living your Bucket List and put your own oxygen mask on. I believe sometimes the best remedy for dark times is to put light into someone else's life! Not only did I help up to 3 people by donating, I got to talk to so many other people about their walks in life and inspire others to start acting Kindly. In addition, my mom surprised me and brought my 9-year-old niece Vada up to see me donate. Vada is terrified of blood and needles and came up to me and said, 'Tia, (what she calls me), I am conquering my fear right now by watching you'...So the journey continues...I left a legacy in my niece's heart! (the 'L' in the Bucket List). There are big ticks and little ticks and your never know how they will impact others!

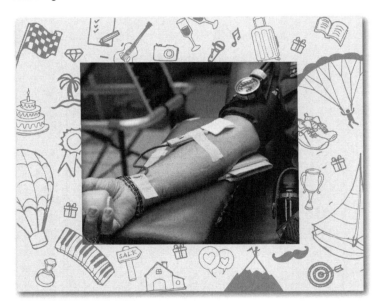

How did you tick it off?

Donating blood is a relatively easy kind act after you get through the hurdles that you need to (fear, education, etc.). It is not something that you have to spend money on or search long and hard to find somewhere to do it, like some other acts of kindness sometimes require. What it does is leaves such warmth in your heart when you do this act of kindness for others. Time is the ultimate currency. None of us know how much time we have but by donating just a little bit of time and blood we give people the gift of life and so much more time. Time with their families, friends and time for others to continue to make a positive impact on this world and the butterfly effect continues!

After donating I felt so much...

Brave — even though I was terrified I knew that I would be okay but the effect I just had on someone else (or 3 people) was potentially life-saving. Conquering fear helps you grow!

Humbled — thinking of all the people who had to care for my mom in the hospital and how much time they had to learn how to care for her. The nurse who checked me in explained she donated for years and years but now she can no longer donate. When she was diagnosed with cancer a few years ago she had to have a blood transfusion and she was on the receiving end — wow! What a story in itself! When I told some of the others donating and nurses helping that I was ticking something off my Bucket List I also opened up their minds to realize that Living a Bucket List Lifestyle was so much more than travel...it is helping you reach your potential and push you in so many different areas that leave a lasting effect on others.

One more feeling I felt was loved — loved by my niece who thinks I am amazing for doing this; loved by the others who were there listening to me; loved by those who saw my post on Facebook and shared their stories and I felt hope for humanity! So many of the people who were there were volunteering their time at the Red Cross to save others. Again, sometimes the best remedy for dark times is to put light in someone else's life!

50 IDEAS TO DO AS KIND ACTS FOR OTHERS

- Raise $250,000 for Amnesty International
- Help out in a soup kitchen
- Be a hospital clown
- Donate blood regularly
- Create a free hugs day
- Sponsor a child from another country
- Donate your time and money to a charity
- Raise awareness for a charity
- Donate your time to an orphanage
- Send a message in a bottle
- Become a volunteer lifesaver
- Become a volunteer fire-fighter
- Volunteer at your local primary school
- Volunteer at a nursing home
- Assist elderly neighbours
- Knit and donate blankets
- Install a 'Before I die wall' in your town
- Donate to your local sporting clubs
- Start a charity that you are passionate about
- Take part in the World's Greatest Shave
- Take part in the 40-hour Famine
- Help others travel the world
- Help with the local Meals-On-Wheels
- Donate your hair for alopecia/cancer sufferers
- Babysit for friends
- Be a Big Brother or Big Sister
- Help organise a dawn service for Veterans

VOLUNTEER FOR A LOCAL CLUB

- Lead a 'Clean Up Day' in your local town
- Host a memorable dinner party for 20 friends
- Cycle for charity
- Feed the homeless
- Offer opportunities to ex-prisoners
- Get involved in a youth leadership program
- Foster animal shelter cats and dogs
- Volunteer with a wildlife rescue service
- Volunteer with your local sporting club
- Give a large anonymous donation
- Crowd-fund for a non-for-profit
- Dedicate a song on the radio to a loved one
- Help a neighbour with a project
- Take your elderly neighbour's rubbish out weekly
- Donate blood
- Leave a 100% tip
- Pay for a family's shopping cart at Christmas
- Leave a $100 dollar note in the library
- Buy a car for someone in need
- Give out gifts to the homeless on Christmas
- Help an elderly person cross a street
- Provide the house deposit for your kid's first house
- Surprise your mother/wife with a clean house

FEED THE
HOMELESS

YOUR TURN

My Kind Acts For Others will be:

TIP

1. Be a nice person (I've assumed that you already are). Being nice is NOT a Bucket List item; it's a character trait. Practise being nicer today than you were yesterday.

2. Get involved with your local community. Start locally to go globally. What can you do within your local community today? Send a message now!

3. Zero in on the one thing that pisses you off that you can do something about and do it; this may also become a Leave A Legacy item.

E: EXPRESS YOURSELF

"EXPRESS YOURSELF,
DON'T REPRESS YOURSELF."
— MADONNA —

How can you express your personal creativity?

What is an extension of you that you could put out into the world?

What did you used to love doing?

What do you find flow in? Where time seems to stop and makes you happy.

What is it about you that you have trouble expressing?

How do you want to be defined by others?

EXPRESS YOURSELF
TRAV BELL

WHAT was your Bucket List item?
Design my own tattoo.

WHY did you want to tick this off?
I really wanted to design something that meant a lot to me. Plus, I was due for a new tattoo. So, I got a tree tattoo on my left calf. As a 'greeny' (environmentally conscious person), growing up at the beach, I've always cared about nature.

The Oak tree is the strongest tree in the world. I use the Oak tree as a metaphor when I teach personal development. What you see above the surface of an Oak tree is exactly what you would see under the ground. Under the ground, hidden from public view is our mindset. The elements of water and sun feed the tree. Just like personal development does for a person's mindset. What you learn and the people you surround yourself with feed you. It makes you strong or weak. The tree is a reminder of all of this for me.

If the roots of a tree are rotten, the tree won't grow, and it won't be very resilient in the wind or in the elements of any storm; which is kind of like life. As a Coach, I know that beliefs (like roots of a tree) can be replaced by new ones. Behavioural patterns, new ways of thinking, lead to growth. My wish for everyone is that they have a strong root system. A strong mindset. So, when we surface and face the world, we are resilient. The trunk represents us...the leader in our own life. The branches on the tree represent different aspects of our life, i.e.: relationships, money, health, vocation. How strong the branches are depends on how strong the trunk is. How strong the trunk is depends on how strong the root system or mindset of the person is.

How did you tick this off your Bucket List?

Firstly, I had to draw up an outline of what I wanted. Being a frustrated graphic artist, I ended up taking my design into the tattooist. I knew exactly where I wanted it and what I wanted. He put the finishing touches to it. The appointment was made and three hours of pain later, it was done. Having it permanently on me is a constant reminder to keep growing in myself. It still serves as a representative anchor every day.

It's made me want to get more meaningful tattoos.

EXPRESS YOURSELF
RODRIGO G. ESCOBEDO SOTO

WHAT was your Bucket List item?

Write and publish my first book.

WHY did you want to tick this off?

I'm a huge fan of Heavy Metal music. I go to a lot of rock and heavy metal concerts. In 2016 I saw a Swedish band called 'Ghost'. They looked scary, had demon masks on and the full antichrist vibe. Their lyrics were full of melody... easy listening for a metal band! There was a lot of beauty in their music. I felt connected. As a result, I had a revelation. (Could have been the beer though!)

I used to blame others for what was wrong in my life. But rather than being a victim, I am more focused on helping others now. My book is related to this. I really love to inspire outsiders. People who feel like they don't belong in this world, who feel completely different. People who don't want to go with the flow, who want to break the monotony, who are sick of doing the same thing every day, are my target audience.

HOW did you tick this off your Bucket List?

I am someone who always makes his goals a reality. The down side of this is that I normally take a long time to tick these things off. I decided I was going to write this book around mid 2016. I started writing it around November 2016. In 18 months, I'd written a total of 80 pages, size 11, full text. When I was at the Bucket List Coach Training, Trav told us to make a commitment towards an important goal in what we Bucket List Coaches call, 'The Countdown'. It's an awesome process. During 'The Countdown', I made myself accountable by messaging my friends and family that I would finish the draft of my book. I'd been putting it off for 2 years.

The social pressure made me massively accountable. I wrote the next 60 pages in 2 weeks. I finished this draft and then got an editor straight away because I wanted to get it published by July 2019. If something is really important to you and you keep delaying, telling people about a deadline can work.

'LIARKDIEL — An angel of light that dominated shadows'...coming to a book store near you!

50 IDEAS TO EXPRESS YOURSELF

- Exhibit your photography
- Collect artwork
- Get a tattoo
- Design your own clothes
- Write a children's book
- Publish your tragedy to triumph story
- Make a documentary
- Create your own quotable quotes
- Invent something
- Put your comic online
- Have a mohawk hairstyle
- Write a poem and publish it
- Write a love song for someone special
- Design a jewellery line
- Create your own website
- Create a photo blog
- Create your own superhero character
- Sculpt something
- Breakdance
- Write a screenplay
- Dress from a different era
- Design handbags
- Design a pair of shoes
- Design your own home
- Get a piercing
- Come out of the closet
- Cook
- Create your own signature dish
- Create your own signature cocktail
- Create your own podcast
- Dress up as a drag queen
- Live truer to your values

GET A MOHAWK

GET A BUCKET LIST TATTOO

DANCE IN THE STREET

- Dye your hair a bright colour
- Sing karaoke
- Paint a picture
- Design a range of pet clothes
- Design a mural on your house
- Write a poem for a loved one
- Quilt
- Photograph your travels
- Create a travel blog
- Create a travel guide

- Present own keynote to 500+ people
- Start a YouTube channel
- Let someone know your true feelings
- Propose in a creative way
- Protest
- Participate in a flash mob
- Start yoga
- Garden

YOUR TURN

My Express Yourself will be:

_____

_____

_____

_____

TIP

1. The first step is to start not giving a fuck
what others think of you.

2. Build and strengthen your 'I don't give a fuck'
muscle starting today.

3. Give yourself serious permission to be
the full expression of you...NOW!

T: TAKE LESSONS

"LIVE AS IF YOU WERE TO DIE TOMORROW.
LEARN AS IF YOU WERE TO LIVE FOREVER."
— MAHATMA GANDHI —

What skills would you love to learn before your time is up?

*Who and (more importantly) what is a skill you've
always been envious of?*

What is that one thing that you've always wanted to be good at?

What's that chip on your shoulder that you need to explore?

*What is something you've wanted to be good at but
never made the time?*

What is something you used to be ok at but need a refresher?

TAKE LESSONS
TRAV BELL

WHAT was your Bucket List Item?
Learn to play chess.

WHY did you want to tick this off?
I'm 45 and I have never known how to play chess. It has always been a chip on my shoulder and I have always wondered how chess worked. Board games were never my thing. So, in the quest to try to do new things, my curiosity got the better of me. Also, I remember watching these old-time 'chess hustler' guys in a Washington Square Park, New York (known as Chess Plaza). Their concentration and move calculations were enviable.

HOW did you tick it this off your Bucket List?
My stepsons gave me a little chess board with little chess

pieces for Christmas. It was actually our first official Christmas together as a family. So, getting this present and the accompanying card was really special. I think I must have mentioned this Bucket List item to them at some stage. So literally, on that very that day, I got taught or should I say 'schooled' in chess. I wasn't taught by some 'Russian uber-chess-nerd' either. Instead, my teacher was my 11-year-old stepson, Darcy.

Getting taught for the first time and playing a match for the first time didn't do a lot for my confidence. Being just a touch competitive didn't help either. Darcy gave me a lot of leeway in the match that we played, and he let me get away with a few things. This resulted in me picking up the rules pretty quickly and thus doing battle on the board. What I thought was going to be a half an hour game, somehow turned into half a day, winner takes all, match. The stress of the match was all worth it. Because I can say we officially drew in my first ever chess game. Proud moment. Darcy is a lovely kid with a heart of gold. Come to think about it, he definitely let me think we drew. I probably owe him another game.

Chess wasn't just fun. It taught me a lot about my own patience. I am very competitive, even with my 11-year-old stepson. I still wanted to 'wipe the floor' with him. But the experience helped me realise that I have a lot more patience than I give myself credit for.

TAKE LESSONS
ROBERT ADDIE

WHAT was your Bucket List item?

Learn about indigenous cultures.

WHY did you want to tick this off?

My time in the Unites States Army as an infantry soldier helped me to understand that there is a big vast world out there. It also taught me that conflict resolution could be done in a different way. Love and understanding were better than invasion and war.

HOW did you tick this item off your Bucket List?

The first step was to leave Key West, Florida and, on faith, arrive in Anchorage, Alaska. I had no vehicle, no job, no housing. This was 1987, so there was no internet, no Facebook and no Google yet. Heck, I had to go down to the local pub and meet people…old school networking! I quickly found some work and crashed on a new friends' couch.

Fast forwards one year, I left Alaska after experiencing the indigenous culture up there. Now, I find myself travelling through the North, South, East and West of Europe, as well as the UK, North Africa and the Arabian Peninsula. I had been living with countless indigenous peoples along the way and have been experiencing an incredible diversity of cultures. Just as planned, my understanding of others has grown. Then, I landed in Nairobi, Kenya and set out to live with the Maasai Warriors tribe. Here is where the real lesson was learned.

As Americans, we don't travel much. So, you can imagine my surprise when a red cloaked, over 6-foot-tall, Maasai Warrior man with red mud-covered braided hair reached out to hold my hand as we walked for the first time to a local water well. His smile and commanding presence were overwhelming. Walking hand-in-hand with another man was frowned upon in many cultures. But among the Maasai, it was a sign of friendship and respect. They are such elegant beautiful people.

As we walked, we came upon a young woman who had the most beautiful golden eyes I had ever seen. She had a spiritual presence. She also had a lot of raised scars and a severe cleft lip. Yet, she carried herself with extreme poise and amazing grace. She had no shame, no hidden face, no cast down eyes. My Warrior friend greeted her with obvious dignity. I asked about the scars and their significance. He told me, 'The magic makes her beautiful'. Meaning, they believed that the disfigurement was special. She was touched by God.

The opposites in Africa forever changed me. 30 years on, I still seek to live a fulfilling, expansive life.

50 IDEAS TO TAKE LESSONS

- Reading and writing
- Tango
- Singing
- Beatboxing
- Ballroom dancing
- Ukulele
- Flying a plane or helicopter
- Cheese making
- Bongos
- Didgeridoo
- Tap dancing
- DJ
- Self defence
- Poker
- Surfing
- Skateboarding
- BJJ
- Breakdancing
- A language
- Wine making
- Acting
- Guitar
- Drums

ARCHERY LESSONS

- Harmonica
- Harp
- Balloon animals
- Knitting
- Public speaking
- Calligraphy
- Journalism
- Radio announcing
- Ice skating
- Bull riding
- Sheep shearing
- Floristry
- Swimming
- Bookkeeping

- Makeup artistry
- Horse-riding
- Dog grooming
- Movie making
- Whip cracking
- 1st Aid

- Sushi making
- Bee keeping
- Paragliding
- Gardening
- Falconry
- Life drawing
- Knife throwing

LEARN TO PLAY AN INSTRUMENT

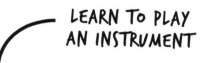

LEARN FLY FISHING

YOUR TURN

My Take Lessons will be:

TIP

1. Ask yourself: What could I 'skill-up' in to help my family?

2. Ask yourself: What could I 'skill-up' in to help my career or business?

3. Ask yourself: What could I 'skill-up' in now that would positively influence the rest of the 11 M.Y.B.U.C.K.E.T.L.I.S.T. Blueprint™ categories?

L: LEAVE A LEGACY

"PLEASE THINK ABOUT YOUR LEGACY BECAUSE
YOU ARE WRITING IT EVERY DAY."
— GARY VAYNERCHUK —

How do you want to be remembered?

What do you want to be remembered for?

*How do you want to be talked about 10, 50,
100 years after you're gone?*

What are you going to leave behind for your family?

What can you start creating now?

What impact can you have and how many people can it help?

LEAVE A LEGACY
TRAV BELL

WHAT was your Bucket List Item?

Create a global network of Certified Bucket List Coaches®.

WHY did you want to tick it off?

As 'The Bucket List Guy' for the last 10 years I have helped a lot of people and their families. The Bucket List message has helped them live with more meaning, purpose and fulfilment. I am also very conscious of the fact that I can only get around the world and see so many people in my lifetime. As a speaker, this has always been a chip on my shoulder and being a big visionary kind of person, that doesn't correlate too well. I want to play a bigger game and impact as many people as I possibly can whilst I'm here.

HOW did you tick it off?

Seneca said, *'Luck is what happens when preparation meets opportunity.'* It wasn't until I gave a talk at the ActionCOACH Global Conference 3 years ago in South Africa that this mission began to take shape. I gave an extended version of my Bucket List Keynote presentation. After my talk, the Founder of ActionCOACH invited me to their headquarters in Las Vegas to talk about licensing my Bucket List philosophy. ActionCOACH have a 1000+ business coaches worldwide in 70+ countries, and growing, at the time of writing.

15 minutes into our meeting we had a business plan mapped out. We would be partners in Certified Bucket List Coach® and I'd be appointed the Global CEO. The Vision we crafted (which is as strong and as top-of-mind as ever) is 'To Create a Purposely Fulfilled World' and our Mission is 'To Help 10 Million Bucket Listers Live Purposely Fulfilled Lives.'

With the help of this strategic partnership, this Bucket List item and the amount of people we can help is really coming to fruition. It's still building, and we are starting to help more and more people around the world every single day. It is really heartwarming. Seeing our hand-selected, compassionate coaches get real results for clients is super cool.

We are on a mission to make life coaching more tangible and not so wishy-washy. We are rebranding life coaching to Bucket List Coaching. Our #tickitB4Ukickit movement is getting more and more traction in countries that I would never have imagined. It's even working in countries where the words 'Bucket List', when translated, don't even make sense!

LEAVE A LEGACY
GLEN THORNTON

WHAT was your Bucket List Item?

Establish the Hugs 4 Change movement.

WHY did you want to tick it off?

I put this on my Bucket List after attending Trav's Bucket List Xperience back in 2012. At the event, I learnt about Trav's M.Y.B.U.C.K.E.T.L.I.S.T. Blueprint™. In particular, the letter L, which stands for Leave A Legacy. For almost 3 years I pondered what my legacy was going to be. It wasn't until I saw a YouTube clip of a guy giving out free hugs blindfolded on the street, that I answered my own question.

Initially I thought I could donate some time and money to a charity of my choosing, but I wanted to create something...from me. Hugs 4 Change came from a passion of wanting to help others and wanting to leave a legacy behind that could continue to help others for many years to come.

HOW did you tick it off?

It seemed that people only did the free hugs thing as a once off according to my YouTube research. I wanted to do it more consistently; once a month, at least. So, I did it. I told no one. I asked a mate to video me without even telling him what was going on. I turned up with a sign that read 'FREE HUGS' and a blindfold and off I went. The blindfold basically tells the public that it doesn't matter who they are, where they are from, what age, race, sex or religion they are...I'll still hug them. The message behind the message is to give love regardless.

By continually doing this, I have started to build awareness and the responses have been overwhelming and absolutely amazing. My plan now is to turn the movement into a legal charity to raise money for Ronald McDonald House and Bear Cottage. Hugs 4 Change Ambassadors around the world are now being established and a national and international Hugs 4 Change Day will be created. To give 1 million hugs and raise 1 million dollars would be a dream realised.

5O IDEAS TO LEAVE A LEGACY

- Plant a tree
- Plant a forest
- Build an eco-village
- Build a school
- Develop a philosophy
- Pass down a personal journal
- Add to the knowledge pool in your field
- Continually contribute to a personal charity
- Leave a property portfolio
- Leave a successful business for your family
- Start a charitable foundation
- Create a Family Trust
- Create a Grant
- Register as an organ donor
- Publish an autobiography
- Trace your genealogy to hand down
- Be a mensch
- Teach your children lessons
- Lead a company to success
- Have an educational facility named after you
- Have a medical facility named after you
- Leave your artwork to someone
- Write books, articles, blogs
- Invent something to help humans live better
- Save an animal species from extinction
- Have a community award named after you

TRACE YOUR GENEALOGY

PLANT A TREE

- Leave a body of research for a disease
- Create an annual father and son event
- Setup a fostering program for animals
- Bequeath your wealth to an animal shelter
- Restore historic architecture
- Create a series of inspirational quotes
- Record timeless music
- Invest in an innovative tech company
- Create a family tradition
- Establish a youth leadership camp
- Create a not-for-profit organisation
- Pass down a family heirloom

- Create an annual fundraising event
- Fight for change at your work
- Create a sustainable and/or fair-trade business
- Fight for women's rights
- Change a policy
- Support a young person's dreams
- Inspire someone to improve their life
- Help someone escape an abusive relationship
- Commemorate by creating a National Day
- Bequeath a family recipe book
- Scrapbook your children's lives then gift it to them on significant birthdays
- Create a lasting mentoring program

YOUR TURN

My Leave A Legacy will be:

....

....

....

....

....

TIP

PLEASE, PLEASE, PLEASE talk this category over with your partner for a) ideas and b) their involvement — so you can both work towards creating something special.

19

I: IDIOTIC STUFF

"YOU DON'T STOP HAVING FUN WHEN
YOU GET OLD, YOU GET OLD WHEN
YOU STOP HAVING FUN."
— RITU GHATOUREY —

What could you just say YES to?

*What are some of random, dumb and silly
things that make you laugh?*

*What's something outrageously out of character
that you'd love to try?*

*What's that thing you've always said,
'that would be fun to do'?*

What would the backpacker in you love to do?

What would you like to surprise people by doing?

IDIOTIC STUFF
TRAV BELL

WHAT was your Bucket List Item?
Smoke a Cuban cigar in Cuba.

WHY did you want to tick it off?
I've always wanted to go to Cuba, it has always fascinated me. I wanted to get there before they started running ferries in to Havana from Key West, Florida. A new flood of tourists could quickly spoil it. There was this certain romanticism and mystery about it, particularly because it had been closed off to American tourism and big investment for so long. Cuba has had an American embargo since 1962 and as a Communist country, it intrigued me. It was just always one of those countries that was hard to get into too. Seeing other people go to Cuba gave me severe F.O.M.O. (Fear of Missing Out). I wrote 'Smoke a Cuban cigar in Cuba' on my Bucket List five years before it happened. A window of time presented itself after visiting Cancun in Mexico, so I figured I was too close, not to tick this one off the List.

HOW did you tick it off?
This was a real mission. Having just done New Year's Eve in Cancun, Mexico, and then (on a whim) buying tickets into Cuba wasn't a smart move. They were very limited and very expensive tickets. We landed in Havana on a one-way ticket at 10pm unable to speak Spanish, with no accommodation booked. At the time, there weren't a lot of hotels or Airbnb's advertised online. So, on arrival, a woman came up to us and asked whether we had accommodation, and when we said no, she said, 'Come with me!'. I was totally suspicious of her, but the people

around us said she was legit. Having limited options, we jumped in a random truck which took us to a 'Casa' that she managed. This place was straight from the 1960s. For $40 USD a night, we scored. Thanks, random lady at the airport at 10pm!

Apart from sightseeing, what do people do in Cuba? In every second picture I Googled they were smoking cigars. The vintage cars, salsa dancing and Havana Club rum were up there too. So, after losing my ATM card in a dodgy machine and having hardly any internet at our disposal, I made my way to the Cuban Cigar Museum. I bought a big fat one, had a very detailed lesson on how to cut it, light it, smoke it and look cool doing it...or so I thought. Selfies all the way. I was now as close to Tony Montana from Scarface as I'd ever get!

As an asthmatic (who's been hospitalised four times for this condition), this was one of the dumbest things I have ever done. I seriously felt ill afterwards and, I guess, in hindsight, the partnering Cuban rum probably didn't help the situation. A rum-soaked night with some very bad salsa dancing followed. It was incredibly fulfilling, and I've never smoked a cigar since.

IDIOTIC STUFF
AARON YOUNG

WHAT was your Bucket List Item?
Rap 'Ice Ice Baby' with Vanilla Ice.

WHY did you want to tick this off?
The build-up to this was huge. I spent the majority of my teenage years rapping 'Ice Ice Baby' in my backyard and in front of the mirror (I mean, who didn't, right?). So, you can imagine, when the opportunity arose, I couldn't control my excitement. Plus, now as a proud father, I get to embarrass my daughters every time this song comes on the radio or at a party. They're actually not that impressed that I know all of the words.

At the time, I didn't have an official Bucket List. However, in the week before the event, my wife and I joked that 'it would be a dream come true' and 'I would die a happy man' if I got to rap 'Ice Ice Baby' with Vanilla Ice.

HOW did you tick this off your Bucket List?
It all happened at the 'I Love The 90s Tour' in Brisbane, June 2017. Concert tickets were only $90, and I was totally committed! To make the dream happen, it required a little bit of help. My brother is a sound engineer who knew the

crew who were working that night. So, we asked a favour and it came through...YES!

We were on stage for about 10 minutes, so I was able to slow down and really enjoy the moment. This really made the experience one to remember. The easiest way to describe it was; that it was like the best party ever. The next morning, I had to check my phone images to make sure that it really had happened. The other fun part was sending the photo to my teenage mates with the tagline 'Dreams Came True Last Night!' I think you can imagine their response.

After ticking this off I immediately wanted to experience this again. So, I added 'Rap 8 Mile with Eminem' to my Bucket List! This experience, along with Trav's talk, has made me realise the importance of a Bucket List and furthermore, how important formalising it is.

50 IDEAS FOR IDIOTIC STUFF

- Cheese rolling in Gloucestershire
- La Tomatina
- Ride the worlds top 20 roller coasters
- Stage dive
- Be a contestant on a TV game show
- Follow the paparazzi for a week
- Board down a live volcano
- Ride a mechanical bull wearing a cowboy hat
- Ride an ostrich
- Ride the world's longest rollercoaster
- Compete in Nathan's Hot Dog Eating Contest
- Skinny dip
- Streak
- Compete in a jousting contest
- Go to Comic-Con as your favourite character
- Fire walk

- Pat a panda
- Create a viral video
- Create a one-hit wonder
- Go on X-Factor
- Go to a rave
- Play paintball in bathers
- Wear a onesie
- Enter in a wife carrying obstacle track contest
- Mud wrestle
- Coordinate a flash mob dance
- Post a World Record on recordsetter.com
- Wrestle your partner in inflatable sumo suits
- Go Zorbing
- Eat the world's hottest chilli

BUSK IN THE STREET

- Go on the annual Zombie Walk in Melbourne
- Do a nudie run through Times Square
- Sing Barbie Girl at karaoke
- Go to a goth nightclub dressed as a fairy
- Dance on big screen at a baseball game
- Recreate the ship scene from Titanic
- Crash a wedding
- Eat a chicken kiev in Kiev, Hungary
- Make a Buckingham Palace guard laugh

- Be a mascot for a sports team
- Host a big party to have a food fight
- Host a mini stage hypnotherapy
- Silent retreat for a week
- 30-day water fast
- Drive 200 kilometres an hour on a racetrack
- Cliff dive at least 50ft
- Drift a car in Japan
- Go to a subway underwear event
- Create a 30 day photobomb challenge with a friend
- Compete in a food eating challenge

GLOUCESTERSHIRE ROLLING CHEESE FESTIVAL[7]

YOUR TURN

My Idiotic Stuff will be:

_____

_____

_____

_____

_____

TIP

1. Organise some drinks with friends today
and ask them for some idiotic tips.

2. Involve them.

3. Set dates and put into your calendar ASAP.

S: SATISFY A CURIOSITY

"A MAN SHOULD LIVE IF ONLY TO
SATISFY HIS CURIOSITY."
— **YIDDISH PROVERB** —

*What would you like to see, taste, touch, smell or
feel before your time is up?*

What would you really like to experience?

What has always had you wondering?

What would you like to find out about yourself?

What are you curious about?

What do you think you could do if you tried?

SATISFY A CURIOSITY
TRAV BELL

WHAT was your Bucket List Item?

See an active volcano.

WHY did you want to tick it off?

I saw a story about the volcano on 60 Minutes. The reporter joined a team of New Zealand adventurers who abseiled into the crater of the volcano down towards the exploding lava below. The fact that this volcano was far from dormant fascinated me and spiked my curiosity from there on. I felt I had to see it. To add to that, I'd never been to Vanuatu either.

HOW did you tick it off?

I finally ticked this off on Tanna Island, which is one of the islands of Vanuatu, after it being on my Bucket List for 3 years.

To get to Vanuatu, I had to organise time out of my personal training business that I owned at the time. So therefore, I had to instruct my managers to take-over the day-to-day operations. My wife, at the time, had to organise time off too because she wanted to come as well...more for the beaches of Vanuatu though, I think! We had to book and pay for flights, accommodation and arrange the extra flights over to Tanna Island from Port Vila, which is the capital of Vanuatu on the main island of Efate.

The journey to get to the volcano was as good, if not better, than seeing the volcano itself! To get to Mount Yasur, you need to endure a pretty tough-going 4WD trip through the forest to get to the base of the volcano. Along the journey, we visited local tribal markets where locals had made and sold hand-crafts and food for the tourists. We also visited a local not-for-profit school and gave gifts to the kids.

After you clear the forest, you come out onto the open black volcano planes at the immediate base of the volcano. It was incredible flying over these swooping black dunes... hanging on for our lives in the back of the 4WD. We went fast. In that moment, I forgot that the driver probably did this drive 4 times a day. I thought it was his first time and that he was out of control. I discovered why there are so many handles built into 4WD drive cars that day!

When we arrived a sign saying, 'Think Safety' greeted us. That was it. It was at the base of a make-your-own-way path to the top of the volcano crater edge. No hand-railing, defined path or even instructions until we completed the 100m walk. The path and the crater edge were littered with black boulders and the stench of sulphur dioxide was overwhelming. It was then when we received our safety instructions. Our guide literally said, 'If big explode (with accompanying hand-gesture), you run. Don't look up, you look down so don't trip'. Even in broken English, he got his point across.

Apparently, that volcano erupts very regularly, and it can send fresh lava and rock flying unpredictably into the air and to where our 'viewing platform' was. More people get hurt by tripping, rather than via the rock and lava shower. He then pointed to a giant boulder that was a solid 1m by 1m cube and said 'that new. Was not here yesterday'. We were now on high alert.

The wind on the day was crazy and there was a constant loud roar. They gave us all bright yellow jackets to protect our clothes from the ash and so we could see each other too. We were told that the best time to go was at dusk. The creeping darkness and the black backdrop of the crater made for a more spectacular lava eruption show. They were right! It was amazing to finally peer over the crater edge, see the constant explosions and see the lava pool at the bottom in between the mini-explosions. It was incredible to see live. It's one thing seeing it on TV, but it's another thing seeing it live. This way, you can really feel it.

This is still a great memory. Recalling it here has been a great trip down memory lane. This (as well as some of the other experiences I've had) has taught me to simply go on gut feeling. If it looks like fun or peaks my interest for more than 24 hours, then there's something in it and it's worth putting on my Bucket List. It's taught me to just book it to make it actually happen. And, to seek out the alternative things to do in this world that may be off the tourist track.

SATISFY A CURIOSITY
MARTY ELBERG

WHAT was your Bucket List Item?
Discover my heritage and my biological relatives.

WHY did you want to tick it off?
I wanted to tick this off my list because I am adopted and wanted to know a bit about my heritage. I was adopted and raised by a very Norwegian mother and a very Swedish father (his parents were direct immigrants).

Although we didn't grow up speaking with an accent and our parents didn't speak much of the language, we were steeped in Scandinavian culture growing up in Iowa. A lot of the Scandinavian immigrants moved to the Midwest when they arrived. It has a similar climate and required hard work, something they were used to in their old country.

I have been lucky enough to visit my family in Norway a few times and have met a few from Sweden. They accept me as a true blood relative and I am very grateful and accept them as true family as well.

Growing up, I always knew I was adopted. My mother would read a book about being adopted to me quite often, so it was never a shock or surprise. I have met several other adoptees who have had a very different experience. Some didn't find out until they were 18, others a bit younger. Many have reported an emotional loss, or feeling of missing out, or even outright betrayal from their adopted parents. I am fortunate enough to have had none of those feelings. Quite the opposite, in fact. I had a good upbringing in a very caring and supportive family. I learned to value family, kindness, a good work ethic and honesty. I didn't and still don't have a 'hole' or sense of missing anything in my life, only a curiosity.

When I initially wrote my Bucket List, I didn't include the DNA test. After some time passed and I ticked several things off of several categories, I revisited my list. I had already satisfied so many curiosities, I was running short on ideas. Turning 50 played a factor in adding the test to my list, especially with the publicity Ancestry.com was getting at the time. People (including public figures) were finding out they had heritage they never even thought of and some took the test to prove their assertions.

I guess 50 was the mile stone I needed to finally satisfy my curiosity of my heritage and see if I could find any biological relatives.

HOW did you tick it off?

A few weeks after I wrote 'DNA' on my Bucket List, I ordered the kit. I received the kit, read the instructions and sent in my sample. All the while my curiosity was even stronger and more intense than ever. When I went online to enter my kit information, the site has an upsell, of course. The upsell was to get connected to DNA matches. That is when I really decided to kick up my 'tick' and see if it was possible to find my biological family members, so I purchased the upgrade.

When the results were in, I clicked in anticipation, and bam my life's perception of reality was turned upside down. Not in a bad way, just in a way I hadn't expected. I am only 5% Swedish and 0% Norwegian. Turns out, I am mostly English, Welsh, Irish, Scottish and German. My DNA profile barely went south of Northern Germany. I had new visions of visiting my DNA homeland knowing 'what' I was. 30 years ago, I lived in London for a few months as a visiting college student and hadn't given it one thought. I wonder what my perception would have been had I known then. First of all, the technology wasn't around then, and I didn't really care that much, so I have no regrets.

What happened next is something that I will never forget. A day later, someone wrote to me on the Ancestry message board and asked about my parents. I had no idea who this person was or how she even saw my results (I didn't explore the site after seeing my results or I may have found out how). She was simply writing to fill in the family tree. I let her know I was adopted and didn't have any family information. She replied saying I should reach out to Linda because she had been writing a family history.

So, I did, and this is what I received:

'Hi Marty — Your message has been anticipated for a few years since I signed on with Ancestry and further, given my DNA. Thank you for writing, I am your birth mother.

Many emotions have surfaced, my decision to adopt you was difficult and I know for the circumstances in 1968, placing you with caring family was the right decision. I have hoped and prayed through the years that you have had a good life.'

Shocked, amazed, bewildered, excited, concerned, disbelief, and a pure WTF (What the F$%#) were a few of the emotions I felt when I first read that message.

I now have two amazing families. My mother is very happy I was able to find my biological mother. My biological mother got an amazing Thanksgiving knowing I was well. Where this story ends, a new one shall begin.

It is definitely not about the list. It is about who you become on the other side of ticking something off the list! Take action and live life!

The Beginning!

SEE THE STATUE OF DAVID IN FLORENCE, ITALY

50 IDEAS TO SATISFY A CURIOSITY

- Enrol in a philosophy course
- Pat a panda
- Have sex with the same sex
- Taste a snow egg
- Ride an elephant
- Master Japanese rope tying
- Map your family tree
- Experience a monk ceremony in Tibet
- Sleep in an ice hotel for a night
- Experience the Burning Man Festival
- Jelly wrestle
- Deliver a baby
- Attend the Olympics
- Sleep in a castle
- Ride a unicycle
- Get DNA tested
- Float in the dead sea
- Space travel to Mars
- Do a Kava ceremony in Fiji
- Feel a porcupine
- Ride a camel in the Arabian desert
- Taste pizza and gelato in Rome
- Ride the Orient Express
- See the northern lights
- Take a helicopter ride
- Watch the birth of an animal

TAKE A HELICOPTER RIDE

GO "FULL KILT"

- If you are a man dress as a woman for a day
- Be on a float at the Carnival in Rio De Janeiro
- Discover your ancestors
- Be an extra in a Bollywood movie
- Live off the land for a week/month
- Go to Wonderland Festival
- Learn to Scuba dive
- See a Tibetan Buddhist sky burial
- Float in a flotation tank
- Go cage shark diving in South Africa
- Drive a Lamborghini around a race track
- Indulge in a bottle of wine in Tuscany

- Explore bondage in a BDSM club
- Attend a Papal mass service at the Vatican
- Experience a geisha tea ceremony in Kyoto
- Dance the tango in Argentina
- Experience an Alaskan Husky sledge ride
- Watch the birth of a human
- Smoke a joint at Bob Marley's house
- Live with no fixed address
- Be the artist drawing a live nude model
- Participate in an Ayahuasca ceremony
- Change your name
- Get a foot spa (fish eating dead skin on feet)

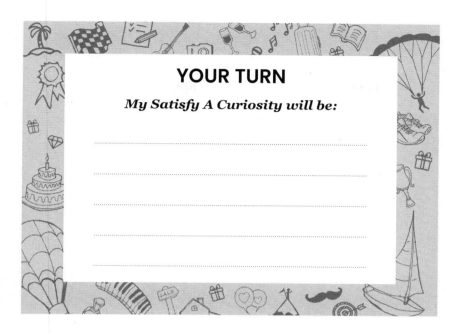

YOUR TURN

My Satisfy A Curiosity will be:

....

....

....

....

TIP

Einstein said
'Curiosity is more important than knowledge'
so take your curiosity seriously.

21

T: TRAVEL ADVENTURES

"THE WORLD IS A BOOK AND THOSE WHO
DO NOT TRAVEL READ ONLY A PAGE."
— SAINT AUGUSTINE —

What's always been on your travel Bucket List?

Where would you love to go if you won the lottery?

What places have you and your family always talked about visiting?

How can you be a tourist in your hometown or own country?

*What are the unique travel experiences
that you'd love to experience?*

What are some of the adventures you'd like to do and who with?

TRAVEL ADVENTURES
TRAV BELL

WHAT was the Bucket List Item?
Celebrate my 40th birthday at Machu Picchu.

WHY did you want to tick this off?
I am on a quest to experience the 7 Man Made Wonders of the World as well as the 7 Natural Wonders of the World. Machu Picchu, being one of the 7 Man Made Wonders of the World has always interested me. As long as I've had a Bucket List, Machu Picchu has been on it, even more than the pyramids.

The famous Inca Trail that finishes at Machu Picchu also held a deep fascination for me. Growing up hiking with my Dad, this hike was on my Bucket List too. To make this even more special, I invited Dad along. I wanted to spend my 40th birthday literally arriving through Sun Gate at

Machu Picchu. Therefore, we had to start the Inca Trail 3 days earlier to make my birthday wish a reality. I've always wondered what it would be like looking down at Machu Picchu. I imagined it would be a very spiritual place. I wasn't wrong.

HOW did you tick this off your Bucket List?

When I started professional speaking, I used to run an event called the Bucket List Xperience. It was a 3-day personal development event. At one of the events, I mentioned to the 50 or so people that Machu Picchu was on my Bucket List and that I was planning on going the year after. Around 10 people said they'd like to join me if I organised it. I wanted to do it in style as it was my 40th birthday too. Therefore, the trip was more 'glamping' than 'camping' and we stayed in 5-Star hotels all the way.

It cost us a small fortune, but it was absolutely amazing. Apart from Dad, my best mate Cam joined us as well as nine other willing Bucket Listers. I'll never forget, on the morning of my 40th birthday, I woke up still on the Inca trail. Our tents were above the clouds. It was silent. The view was amazing. I was 40. We still had a half day to trek.

The chefs and porters made me a 40th birthday cake. Their Spanish rendition of 'Happy Birthday' at 7:30am was so memorable. Watching the video now only brings happy tears. Popping a bottle of champagne at that altitude popped pretty hard too. I can't believe they did this. It was super special.

By about lunch time, we made the 100 steps that lead up in to Sun Gate which looks over Machu Picchu. I was the first up the steps. Finally seeing this vision in person was truly amazing. Of course, I teared-up. It was beautiful.

But when Dad came through...it was one of the first times I've seen him speechless. I will never forget the look on his face. He was in awe. We hugged. It was one of the most memorable moments of my life.

TRAVEL ADVENTURES
DR TROY HENDRICKSON

WHAT *was the item on your Bucket List?*
Take Dad and brother on a fishing trip to Alaska.

WHY *did you want to tick this off your Bucket List?*
One of the things that my father had always talked about was his desire to go to Alaska to go fishing. As an avid fisherman throughout his entire life (he is now 74 years old), it was one of the things that he always dreamed about doing... someday. While attending Trav's Bucket List seminar, I got the 'fire in my belly' to make this trip happen because I realised that at age 74, the potential of that 'someday' never happening was very real, unless I proactively took the steps to make it happen. My sister died from a long battle with cancer just three years earlier in 2010, so the notion of 'taking our life span for granted' really resonated with me when Trav talked about this in the workshop. The idea to take my dad and my brother on this 'Bucket List trip' to Alaska had been planted, and it was germinating very quickly within my mind.

HOW did you tick this off your Bucket List?

Over the next three days I did meticulous research regarding all of the nuances of this Alaska fishing trip, including the best locations to go to, the best fishing guides, the best times and, of course, the best place to actually stay at. If this trip was going to happen, it was going to be special. I knew that I was going to have to ask for forgiveness rather than permission because my father would most certainly have some lame excuse for why he could not go (aches and pains or some other justification/rationale for why it was not a good idea). I also realised that this may be the only time that my father, my brother and I could spend time together experiencing something that was very memorable. I grew up with two siblings and with my sister no longer living, my brother and I are the only 'children' that remain. So, I decided that I needed to also bring my brother on the trip. There was a slight problem...he had never flown on a plane before and he is incredibly afraid of heights. Although there were many obstacles, I was determined to make it happen. I even contacted my brother's boss (without him knowing) to secure the time off in his work schedule so that I could minimise excuses he would present to me. I needed to proactively address any and all obstacles and create a scenario that minimised the likelihood of them having an excuse NOT to go.

Although there was a huge risk in them bowing out, I booked the flights and secured a 7,000-square foot log cabin on the Kenai Peninsula for an entire week in May. I also locked in fishing guides throughout the week so that we could go fishing for king salmon, sockeye salmon, halibut and rainbow trout.

When I contacted my father and brother to inform them of the trip, it was not a request for them to come...it was a demand for them to be a part of my Bucket List adventure.

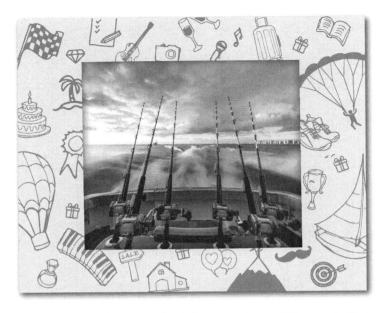

Long story short, we had the most incredible week that I could possibly imagine — catching our limit of every one of the previously mentioned species of fish and having an absolute blast! However, there was one 'moment' that will be etched in my memory forever. I remember glancing over at my dad as he looked out the window of the plane during our fly-in sockeye salmon trip, absorbing the amazing scenery, with his hand resting on my brother's leg...there was a small, glistening tear streaming down his cheek as he said, 'I never thought this would actually happen...especially not with my two sons, this is a dream come true'.

Amidst the hundreds of memorable experiences throughout the week, that one moment made all of the financial investment and time spent preparing the trip 100 per cent worth it. As it turned out, this was not just a Bucket List trip for me...but for my dad and my brother as well. Trav was absolutely right...life is way too short. Don't wait to do the things that you know you want to do!

50 IDEAS FOR TRAVEL ADVENTURES

- Visit every country on earth
- Visit the 7 Natural Wonders of the World
- Visit the 7 New Wonders of the World
- Backpack through Tibet
- Cruise the River Nile
- Do an African Safari
- Visit the Great Wall of China
- Do a Hollywood Tour
- Ride over the Golden Gate Bridge, California
- Visit the Pyramids
- Drive Route 66
- Go into space on Virgin Galactic
- Visit Yellowstone National Park
- Cruise Ha Long Bay, Vietnam
- Swing at the end of the world, Ecuador
- Hike the Inca Trail to Machu Picchu, Peru
- Road trip around Australia
- Be at the Changing of the Guard, Buckingham Palace
- Attend the Day of The Dead Festival in Mexico City
- Go to the Candle Festival Yi Peng Festival in Thailand

- Have a white Christmas in New York
- Run the 'Rocky Stairs' in Philadelphia, USA
- Ride around Central Park in NYC, USA
- Do a Pablo Escobar tour, Medellin, Colombia
- Visit the White House in Washington DC
- Cable-car up Table Mountain, Cape Town
- Swim in the 5 oceans
- Ride in an old car in Havana, Cuba
- Walking with the Lions in Zimbabwe, Africa
- Visit the Bob Marley Museum, Jamaica

- Ride along Venice Beach, California
- Cruise the Mekong Delta River, Vietnam
- Bridge Bungee Jump, Queenstown, NZ
- Walk Sagano Bamboo Forest, Japan
- Attend the world's biggest food festivals
- Track Gorillas, Uganda
- Visit Santa's workshop, North Pole
- Have New Year's Eve in Times Square, NYC
- Ride the Orient Express train
- Travel on the Ghan train
- Ride the Trans-Siberian Railway
- Hot Air Balloon over Cappadocia
- Dive off a cliff into the Mediterranean
- Visit Edinburgh Castle, Scotland
- Drive along the French Riviera
- Go to a tea plantation in Sri Lanka
- Check out Area 51/Alien Highway in New Mexico
- Watch sunrise over Angkor Wat, Cambodia
- Visit Ghandi's house, India
- Walk the salt flats in Bolivia/Chile

YOUR TURN

My Travel Adventures will be:

TIP

1. Be a tourist in your own hometown first. Tick off the small, easy, less expensive options first.

2. Involve your friends and family to create 'good pressure'.

3. Look to combine other Bucket List items while you travel. This gives you an even bigger reason to go!

A BUCKET LIST IS A TANGIBLE LIFE PLAN WHERE YOUR BUSINESS PLAN OR CAREER PLAN SHOULD FIT INTO YOUR LIFE PLAN. **NOT** BE THE OTHER WAY AROUND.

22

TAKE REAL ACTION

"YOU ARE WHAT YOU DO,
NOT WHAT YOU SAY YOU'LL DO."
— CARL JUNG —

Look, after being a personal trainer for so many years, I know how hard it can be to keep your motivation up. I've seen people get all revved up at the start and then (depending on the person's 'why') seen that motivation die off. Personal development is no different. Can you recount the amount of self-help seminars or motivational books you've witnessed or read over the years where you have left feeling 8-foot-tall and bullet-proof, just to have motivational kryptonite appear only days later? I sincerely don't want you to be one of 'those' people.

A word to the wise though, be really careful of what you put on here. Why? Because when the momentum of your Bucket List achievements starts to build, who knows where it may take you. When you start there may be just a few things on this list. Once confidence grows though, you'll get hooked, and you'll add more and more things. Next thing you know, you'll be half way up the North Face of Everest! Also, please be aware of any age limitations you may have. If you're 65 years old and you want to play professionally for the Chicago Bulls NBA team, sorry buddy, 'You must be dreamin'...as they say in the classic Australian film, *The Castle*.

Anyway, as I mentioned at the start of the book, getting going straight away, is a great way to keep hold of that initial drive. That, and working hard to create a snowball effect, are the two best pieces of advice in regard to holding on to your motivation and making sure you're not just another 'one day' wonder.

Accountability is also really important in this process. Who's going to hold you accountable to your Bucket List? Your partner? Your family? Your friends? Unfortunately, some of those people aren't going to be as supportive as others. But don't let that stop you. In the end the best person to keep you accountable is You! It's your life, your Bucket List and, ultimately, your happiness in the balance. It's up to you to make sure it happens. Email your list to my team to keep yourself accountable.

Be aware of self-sabotage during this process too. People's voices can dig into your motivation and make you second guess your choices to fulfil your Bucket List. You might start to question yourself about whether you're being selfish, trying to accomplish things you've always wanted to do. Don't let that change your focus. You absolutely deserve to fulfil your dreams and create a life full of meaning and joy, through ticking off your Bucket List items. That's where the difference between action and procrastination is really important. So here are some ideas to help you do that.

Let's talk about what Taking Real Action does and doesn't look like.

What does ACTION not look like?	What does ACTION really look like?
• A Google search	• Booking a holiday
• Being a 'GUNNA' i.e.: telling someone that you are going to do something	• Engaging other Bucket Listers in one of your items
• Looking up prices for something online, but waiting to book 'until prices are better'	• Paying a non-refundable deposit
• Endless research	• Publicly declaring your plans on social media
• Basically, being all talk.	• Creating a meeting
	• Enlisting personal support to keep you personally accountable
	• Connecting with a group to create social accountability
	• Launching a crowd-funding campaign.

As part of our Bucket List Life Plan program that our Certified Bucket List Coaches® run we ask each participant to Take Action. Real Action! But the best part of this program is that we ask them to show proof of their action. Yes, we basically call 'bullshit' until we see proof. Participants know that they are going to be asked for proof, so our coaches never fail to get results. Accountability plus!

23

THE FUCKIT LIST

Yes, you read it correctly...a Fuck It List.

I was interviewed on a State-wide drive-time radio show recently to join a Bucket List discussion. Basically, I was brought in to clear up some of the definitions and misconceptions around the concept.

Anyway, the other participants were talking about how the idea of Bucket Lists wasn't open to everyone, because for whatever reason, not everyone wants to run a marathon, or climb Kilimanjaro, or swim with Great White sharks. I felt the need to point out that, despite the common misconception, you don't have to have any of those things on your Bucket List. I helped them (and listeners) understand that a Bucket List needs to be personal and holistic. If you see something on someone else's Bucket List that you like, absolutely copy, cheat or steal it. If you see or hear something that is on another's Bucket List and your first response is, 'No thanks! I've got no interest in that whatsoever!' then that is a good sign that rather than belonging on your Future Bucket List, it belongs on your Fuck It List.

As soon as people know you're working on a Bucket List they will try to help. People will throw all kinds of ideas at you that they think you may like to have on your Bucket List. Some will be awesome, and some well, straight to the Fuck It List. These are the ideas that just hold no kind of interest for you, whatsoever.

It's ok to have a Fuck It List. It's important to say no to adding things to your Bucket List that aren't true to who you are. It's your Bucket List after all. Don't get on this journey of living your dreams, just to start living out someone else's Bucket List at the expense of your own. Plus, it's much easier to work out what you really do want to do when you know what you don't want to do.

It's also important to remember that you can move something from the Bucket List to the Fuck It List as time goes on and your priorities change. I've done that with Summiting Everest. I don't need to do that, I've done Advanced Base Camp, I've climbed Kilimanjaro, I don't need to do Everest to prove to myself I'm a good climber. Plus, with my tendency to get awful altitude sickness very easily, the likelihood of me actually making it to the summit is pretty low. So, I've moved it to my Fuck It list, which has freed up time, energy and money to focus on challenges and other Bucket List items that I actually do want to accomplish.

WORK HARD, PLAY HARD

W ell, here we are, at the final stages of ticking this big Bucket List item off my list. Woo hoo! It certainly has been a long time coming. I've promised myself that the next one won't take so long and the fact that I've managed to find a degree of flow at times during the writing of *The M.Y.B.U.C.K.E.T.L.I.S.T. Blueprint*™ indicates that this may not be a one-trick pony after all.

In fact, I have had to take some sizeable chunks out of this book and reserve them for the next one. Those chunks, those ideas, the stories and concepts have now laid a very solid foundation for book number two. Adding to this, too, is the fact that the crowds are getting bigger and bigger at my events and therefore more and more people are being affected, or should I say, infected, by the Bucket List Philosophy. It's so cool to see that the library of real-life results of people changing their lives around me is growing significantly.

So, book number two is going to happen folks and will undoubtedly contain even more stories from Bucket Listers around the world who are out there ticking off the things that help them feel fulfilled. But the next book won't only cater for Bucket List individuals, it will flow out to groups, teams, businesses and corporations. Why can't we expand individual awesomeness to collective awesomeness, right? That's why we have a tribe of Certified Bucket List Coaches® now too - to help the world #tickitb4Ukickit. I'm writing this in 2020 and I can tell you, the world needs some love, laughs and adventure, possibly more than ever before.

I've spoken at a lot of business and industry sectors, from banking to Australian sporting bodies, manufacturing corporations, fitness franchises, education sectors, mining groups and the list goes on. One thing I have noticed is how teams transform and behave differently after they have bonded over their Bucket List. They unite and begin to help each other network, supporting each other in ways to tick things off their list.

Just imagine the massive shift in workplace culture if more employers took time to discover what truly made their employee's hearts sing? Or if the boss actually encouraged staff members to make a Bucket List and helped them tick their items off it. It transforms and revolutionises workplaces and people. It boosts morale and increases togetherness. How do I know? Because I've seen it happen and I intend to make it happen more often!

Of course, it's not rocket science, but when people reveal some of their true personality and deepest dreams, people connect more and get to know each other outside of work. They build more powerful bonds and develop themselves personally and professionally. They become happier team members and bring more zest and smiles to the workplace.

Now, I don't want to end this book on a downer, but I can't manipulate the statistics.

Did you know:

- 79% of employees quit their job due to "lack of appreciation" from their leaders.[8]
- On average, people spend three days in the past month thinking about quitting their job, and more than four days dreading going to work.[9]
- 87% of company recognition programs focus on tenure and have NO impact on performance.[10]
- 69% of Australian employees are not engaged in their jobs.[11]
- An average people spend more time complaining on a Monday morning than any other day of the week. (Roughly, 34 minutes).[12] Yes, they spread Mondayitis to everyone.
- 1 in 5 people in the workplace experience a mental health condition.[13]
- 52% of employees believe their workplace is mentally healthy and only 56% believe their most senior leader values mental health.[14]
- Toxic employees infect the workplace with negativity and are often the reason for other team members to quit their job. Good employees quit at a 54 percent higher rate when they work with a toxic employee.[15]
- The cost of a single toxic employee is approximately $8,800 per year. Thus, the toxic employee costs over three times that of a non-toxic employee.[16]

Now, the stats and studies keep coming thick and fast, but I don't want to depress you. In a nutshell, something is going majorly wrong in the workplace and it's costing people their time, happiness and money. Businesses are suffering too.

- Globally, disengaged employees costs the world economy a staggering $7 trillion dollars in lost productivity. Yes, trillion! 1 billion dollars from the US alone.
- The retention and recruitment costs on average 150% of an average salary to replace a team member.
- Estimates indicate that depression costs US employers $24 billion annually in lost productive work time.
- Unhappy employees take ten times more sick days than happy ones, whereas happy employees have approximately 12% greater productivity.
- Employee engagement gives an average of 21% higher levels of profitability.

The bottom line is everyone wants to live a happy fulfilling life. People want to be happy and engaged with their work. Employers want happy, productive team members. Everybody essentially wants the same thing. So, why is there such a divide between what people want and what they experience, almost on a daily basis?

I believe it's because we all have core human needs that must be met. We need a sense of belonging and an environment that allows us to thrive. We need to feel supported and hold a sense of purpose and individual accomplishment. We want to meet life in all its glory and we need to find a place where this is possible.

Work cultures must adapt and embrace this joy for life and expression. Workplaces aren't jails, they are places for people to grow and bring their strengths to the table. Now I'm not suggesting you bring in the circus every lunch time and engage in juggling and fire throwing activities to bring some fun to the workplace (and I'm not saying that you shouldn't either). I'm talking about deepening your purpose and focus on creating an inclusive workplace that develops people's dreams and sense of belonging and care.

I want to help businesses become the Employer of Choice and help employees increase their joy and motivation. I can guarantee that teams operate better, and with increased productivity, when their morale and purpose is set in motion. As team's tick off their daily to-do list, they can also be ticking their Bucket List. That's why I have created a special *M.Y. B.U.C.K.E.T.L.I.S.T Blueprint for Business*. It outlines many of the requirements a team or business sector needs in order to thrive in today's market. Things like team building, communication, loyalty, energy, engagement and mental health are all taken into account.

To me, this is the future. We aren't working the same way we did 20 years' ago. Leading-edge companies like Google, Facebook and Twitter have pioneered a new way of working. They understand that culture can make or break a business.

Other companies are also seeing that productivity, purpose and being personable are much better all rolled into one. Mega toy-maker LEGO turned their working space into a playground. Their headquarter office is filled with bright colour and building blocks as they encourage their employees to live their company vision of "Inventing the future of play". Yes, you get paid to play at LEGO.

Web hosting mogul GoDaddy have also looked at their workplace culture. They have invested in "fun" like including a basketball court, skate park, sandpit, mini-golf course and a climbing wall to give their employees some space to unwind and play. Less stress, higher productivity.

We've all seen Richard Branson's ability to develop leadership, increase profit and have fun at the same time. And it's not just him — it's his team at large. He understands that putting people in their right zone of genius and giving them space to innovate and connect is vital to growth. In fact, fun for him is essential, not just something that happens once at the end-of-year Christmas party.

Progressive employers are understanding that the new way to build high-performing teams and businesses is by lifting them up and supporting them. And in turn, they'll support you too. It's no wonder that 64% of jobseekers look for a good company culture where employee happiness is just as important as increasing profits. Anyway, more of that in book 2.

The point is – you can work hard and play hard. I do it every day. Truly. It's a way of life that you can create in your home and in the workplace.

If you want Trav to come to your business or group, please go to: https://www.thebucketlistguy.com/speaking

THE PERSON YOU BECOME

I initially embarked on this mission to write *The M.Y.B.U.C.K.E.T.L.I.S.T. Blueprint*™ whilst I was on a Eurorail Fast Train speeding through the German countryside after attending the Eurovision Song Contest final. I was literally in-between two Bucket List ticks at the time. The other was 'To Backpack Around Europe For a Month as a Grown-Up'. Goes to show that you don't have to finish one Bucket List tick before you start another.

On a side note, I want you to layer your Bucket List adventures. Do them consecutively. Have a look at your list and see which ones you can combine. Observe which ones naturally create a platform for the next and let the game of life begin!

Anyway, back to the train in Germany. That's where I started this. But, if you could see me now, I am back where I grew up. As I write these final words, I am sitting at the Dunes Cafe in Ocean Grove, Victoria, Australia. It overlooks Ocean Grove main beach. This is where Dad taught me how to body surf. This is where I learned to save lives as a nipper through the Ocean Grove Surf

Life Saving Club and this is where I tested my first surfboard when I was five years old and never looked back. Talk about having a reflective moment!

But it's obvious, I guess. Seeking adventure has always been a part of my life. I was born into it. Still to this day, Dad and his close mates are still out there, sea-kayaking, camping and hiking. At 70+ years of age, he's still out there discovering new rivers, new tracks and new landscapes. I guess I'm simply paying this sense of adventure forwards and labelling it with the Bucket List brand.

Never in my wildest dreams did I think I'd be a globe-trotting adventurer who speaks to and coaches people and teams around the world for a living and completely loves what he does. I am so grateful to everyone in my life who has helped me shape the path that I am now on. This includes you, the reader of this book.

Writing it has been a very cathartic exercise for me. I'd highly recommend it to anyone. So, if you are considering including 'Write A Book' on your Bucket List then start right now. They say that writing, as well as speaking and coaching is therapy because it allows you to express your thoughts and feelings, rather than having them trapped-up inside you. It's an extension of your identity and of your personality. It has helped me discover more detail in my stories, examples, metaphors, and aided in the development of richer and more meaningful content. As a result, my seminars are fuller and more impactful. Remember… it's about the person you become on the journey to achieving the things on your Bucket List and it's also about the person you discover on the other side of your Bucket List.

SMELLING THE ROSES…AND THANK YOU

From the bottom of my heart, I want to sincerely thank you for reading *The M.Y.B.U.C.K.E.T.L.I.S.T. Blueprint*™. Let it be something that you rip into, write all over, highlight and refer back to. It was originally designed to give you a bunch of Bucket List ideas and to inspire you to live a life by your own design and have no regrets in the end. I've always said, that if you go to a seminar or read a book and you learn just one thing that causes a new decision or inspires a new action to be taken, then it's been worth the time invested in reading or attending. So, I hope you've had at least one 'ah-ha moment'. No actually, I hope you've had several.

I used to live for goals. I was obsessive about the achievement of them. I did whatever I needed to do to succeed in my mission. A lot of the time I delayed my sense of gratification until a goal I set was attained. A lot of people think about goals in the same way. I call it the 'I'll be happy WHEN syndrome'. If this book has taught you anything, I hope it has been for you to be present, be mindful and to smell the roses on your journey.

I liken life to rowing west towards the horizon…you're never going to get there. It's true. But to think about that I don't want you to be disheartened, I want you to be excited. You see because while you're rowing, you'll see islands in the distance on your journey. Some will be close, while others will be far. Some will be big, and others will be small. You'll have to work harder to get to some than you will to others. But overall, each island acts as a motivator for you to row towards. Because every island brings a new realm of discovery and adventure.

Imagine that each island is like a Bucket List item. You'll get there, you'll tick it off your list. You'll pat yourself on the back. You'll experience a sense of achievement and revel in the fact that you've uncovered more of your personal potential that was lying within. But I also know that once ticked, you'll become restless and start to say to yourself, 'ok, what's next?'. You may even find yourself getting used to your new-found destination and becoming complacent. That's when you'll get to the other side of the island and start looking west again. As human beings, we are addicted to growing and developing. It's your birthright to never stop.

My suggestion is to do a new Google Search, get back in your boat and start rowing again. Life is about discovering IT and your place in IT.

But don't for one second forget where you are. Don't just fix your eyes on the next island and row like crazy towards that next Bucket List tick. Stop, slow down and don't obsessively rush around wherever your boat is at any point in the journey, because I bet there's some really amazing things happening all around you. Look at the dolphins, hear the birds and feel how warm that water is. Also, how cool is this boat that you're in? There's a lot going on if you really pay attention.

Enjoying the journey as well as the destination is what this is all about. Smell the roses, but don't stop adding and don't stop ticking. Get busy living and live life with no regrets.

I wish you well on your journey and cannot wait to hear about your Bucket List adventures. But don't dream it, do it! If you'd like to share your Future Bucket List personally with me simply fill out your My Bucket List Blueprint Summary at the end of this book and send it to me.

LIFE IS WAY TOO SHORT NOT TO LIVE YOUR BUCKET LIST.

— Trav Bell (The Bucket List Guy)

P.S - And wait for it...here's the big tick! I did it! I wrote a book. It's ticked off my Bucket List and it feels goooooooddd.

But wait, there's more...

Here's a sneak peak about my next book all about team engagement within business.

COMING SOON!!

IS WRITING A BOOK ON
YOUR BUCKET LIST?

WOULD YOU LIKE TO APPEAR
IN AN UPCOMING BOOK WITH ME,
THE BUCKET LIST GUY AND TICK IT
OFF YOUR LIST ONCE AND FOR ALL?

SUBMIT YOUR BUCKET LIST STORY
AND APPLY TODAY.

GO TO:
DEANPUBLISHING.COM/MYBUCKETLIST

MY BUCKETLIST SUMMARY

Re-write your Future Bucket List items here or submit them to
The Bucket List Guy at https://thebucketlistguy.com/upload-your-list

M **MEET A PERSONAL HERO (PAGE 51)**

Y **YOUR PROUD ACHIEVEMENTS (PAGE 59)**

BUY THAT SPECIAL SOMETHING (PAGE 69)

ULTIMATE CHALLENGES (PAGE 77)

CONQUER A FEAR (PAGE 87)

KIND ACTS FOR OTHERS (PAGE 95)

EXPRESS YOURSELF (PAGE 105)

TAKE LESSONS (PAGE 113)

LEAVE A LEGACY (PAGE 121)

IDIOTIC STUFF (PAGE 129)

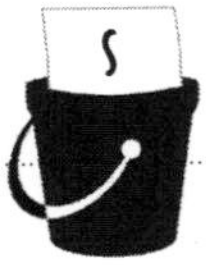

SATISFY A CURIOSITY (PAGE 137)

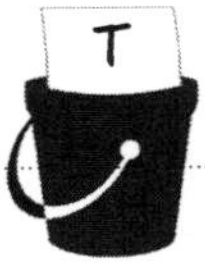

TRAVEL ADVENTURES (PAGE 149)

ACKNOWLEDGEMENTS

Big shout-out to the following people:

My Family — thank you for allowing me to indulge in my obsession. At times, I get way too obsessed. I call it passion...of course! I am so grateful that you are all a part of my life. Leave A Legacy took on a whole new meaning for me when you adopted me as your partner (Tracey) and as your step-dad (Charlie, Jane, James and Darcy). I love you guys.

Travis Beckley — you've been by my side through this whole journey and all my crazy and not-so-crazy ideas. From franchising personal training studios around Australia to this Bucket List Guy idea and now to our Certified Bucket List Coach® global network of coaches. You've been a rock mate and I couldn't have done it without you.

Cam Gill — you lived six or was it seven years past your initial 'use-by date'. Your cancer bought us together as best mates. Your example and attitude (right up until the end) continues to inspire me every single day. We squeezed a lifetime of fun and adventures into the time we had. Cam, mate, I'm looking at your tree from my desk as I write this. I miss you. Thanks for everything bro.

Brad Sugars — thank you validating this idea of mine and helping me to scale it out to the world. You have always been an amazing business coach to me and you continue to be now as a business partner.

Susan Dean — and the rest of the team at Dean Publishing for finally making this happen! Your book coaching, support, ideas and inspiration couldn't have come at a better time. We did it...#tickitB4Ukickit! Now, onto the next one.

Our Certified Bucket List Coach® Tribe — thank you to this crazy, heart-centred bunch. I hope that this book serves as a tool to help you help our clients all around the world. Thank you for trusting us at Bucket List HQ and for investing in the Certified Bucket List Coach® brand and paying the #tickitB4Ukickit movement forward. Together, we are all making our Vision and Mission a reality.

ABOUT THE AUTHOR

From the age of 18 I have written a 'To Do Before I Die' list even though Bucket Lists weren't a thing back then. Thanks to *The Bucket List* movie and the popularity of the concept, they certainly are now. It's a heavily hash tagged and tweeted global phenomenon.

Now as a 40-something-year-old guy, my Bucket List is my reason why I attack life. It has always been my compass, my motivation. It continues to give me purpose and add meaning into my life.

Ignorantly, I thought everyone had a written list like me...but apparently not.

Around 2010, someone called me The Bucket List Guy because of all the crazy and interesting things I'd done in my life up to then (thanks Jo). Since then I have become a world recognised Thought Leader on the topic; hence why I've been crowned 'The World's No.1 Bucket List Expert'.

Instead of letting it be about me and my List though, I've now dedicated my life to helping others wake up and live theirs before it's too late or before they get given a 'use by date'. But it's not just a simple list. It's a fundamental philosophy for life, based on the principles of Positive Psychology, and I am proud to say that our tribe of 'Bucket Listers' are living with more purpose, meaning and fulfillment because of this philosophy.

My Vision is 'My Vision is To Create A Purposefully Fulfilled Word' and my mission is To Help 10 Million Bucket Listers Lead Purposely Fulfilled Lives. I know it's a big call, but I continue to spread my ideas through my podcast, blog, keynote speeches, and I've even ticked off 'Do a Ted Talk' too. Now with the help of my global network of Certified Bucket List Coaches®, we are focused and on track to impact so many more lives. It's what gets us out of bed in the morning.

When not travelling the world, ticking things off my list, I live on Australia's famous Surf Coast, Ocean Grove, Victoria, Australia.

TESTIMONIALS

'Very inspiring – the audience got right into it. They got a lot out of it, very entertaining, very moving and inspiring, LOVED your message.'

Phil Quin Conroy – PLAN Australia

'We have just had the privilege of having Travis present to over 300 tennis coaches on how to live life to the fullest and create a Bucket List life. The coaches are pumped!'

Andrea Buckeridge – Tennis Australia

'We had people laughing and crying in a good way. Really just focusing on what they are wanting to achieve in life. It really shifted a lot of people. I'm hugely grateful Travis.'

Bruce Campbell – Entrepreneurial Business School

'I just wanted to say thank you to Trav for coming down and facilitating our Bulldogs Friendly Business Networking Event. It was a great night. He spoke really well and he had the crowd really engaged. So thank you, I highly recommend him. He was fantastic! Lots of fun and really made everyone get out of their comfort zone. It was a fantastic networking session. Thank you Trav.'

Western Bulldogs

'We had The Bucket List Guy come in today — it made a great session! I got a lot personally out of it. We talked a lot about stepping out of our comfort zone and challenging ourselves and creating the life that we've always wanted. It was just fantastic! Jump on board.'

Toni –Head coach of the Victorian & Tasmanian branch of
The Australian Institute of Fitness (AIF)

'I just had an opportunity to observe Travis Bell in action for one-and-a-half hours at our convention and the guy was just amazing! He had so many things to talk about as far as the tribe is concerned, but most importantly, he got people engaged and standing up. He was giving people a lot of information related to how to build their own type of tribe which is really fantastic. I thought it was really engaging. I was participating, right from the back of the room even though I was seated on my own, but it was good stuff. So, Travis Bell - thank you very much. You did a great job. Thanks for being with us here in Singapore and thanks for coming out here to speak to us. You're awesome man. Thank you.'

Raymond Thomas – entrepreneur, leadership consultant, speaker,
and trainer. Asia Professional Speakers Singapore (APSS)

'Trav delivers great value and brings a fresh and energising perspective to his speaking. I can say that he is truly transformational. My world is better for having worked with him and I know that yours can be also.'

Julie Garland McLellan
https://www.mclellan.com.au

'I had the pleasure of working with Trav on a 1-day event I had organised with clients of mine. It was a risk to bring in another speaker, but he didn't disappoint. My clients loved him and he was a huge hit. His personality and style was fun and engaging. His message and content were relevant and thought-provoking. I have since had feedback from the group that they have implemented many of the time management and goal-setting tools that Trav shared, which is always a good sign of a great speaker with a powerful message.'

Kirsty Spraggon
https://kirstyspraggon.com

'I want to tell you about Trav Bell's speaker program. First of all—it's dynamic. Second of all — it's measurable. Everything you do will have measures against it. Next —it holds you you're accountable, not just to yourself or Trav, but for others in the group as well. Does it work? Trav is living proof that it works. And it's a lot of fun. We had a load of fun ...it's changed my life. So, two things to take away from this: Be visible. Life's too short. Get on with it. Get connected to Trav.'

Gordon Jenkins – The Visible Guy
https://www.iamgordonjenkins.com

'As a former award-winning entrepreneur and lecturer, I have attended many conferences and listen to many speakers. Trav's presentation is not only thought-provoking, entertaining, and informative but LIFE-CHANGING. He is VERY engaging... ABSOLUTELY one of the best speakers I have listened to in 40 years! I would never go out of my way to listen to the same presentation again...but I would for this guy. As a father of eight, I want every one of my 8 kids to hear his presentation.'

Larry Carnell – Nationally Respected Award-Winning Franchise & Funding Expert, Broker, Trainer & Consultant.

'Trav Bell is an incredible visionary delivering an unbelievably important message through his work as The Bucket List Guy. In a world that is getting busier and busier, Trav Bell's message cuts through it all with a straightforward message that comes from deeply held beliefs and experiences in his life. Whether you've met Trav or not, his message cannot help but touch each and every one of us in a way we probably need more than we realise yet.'

Dustin Elliot – Better Questions Better Life and Customer service success manager.

'I saw Trav present on the weekend and he was really engaging and energetic. More importantly, he made me think. If you are looking for a dynamic speaker who will rock your boat in a positive way, I would highly recommend Trav (and I've seen A LOT of speakers).'

Phil Lee — Technology Sales Growth Expert

'Trav has an exceptional way of pushing your comfort zone to achieve incredible results. To say that working with Trav changed my life would be a gross understatement. The impact he has had on my life has been nothing short of amazing. Trav's techniques for goal setting, removing what holds you back and inspiring you to achieve all you can is phenomenal. I highly recommend him as a coach, as a speaker and a human being.'

Teresa Lombardo – Change champion and creative thinker
https://teresalombardo.com

'In the short time I have known Trav he has literally changed my life and that of my family. My dad and I attended Travis Bell's Design your Bucket List events last year and amazing things have happened over and over triggered by this confronting, compelling and motivating event. Spending time with Trav is a no BS wake-up call that I recommend to ALL. I have applied and am applying his Bucket List system and am recruiting family, friends and family to do the same. It has become part of my daily vernacular and behaviour. This process has brought so much energy, vitality and meaning (oh yeah - and FUN) back into my life that I now endeavour to live every day "ON PURPOSE". I LOVE your work Trav - you are an inspiring game-changer and I am a believer - keep working that list mate and leading by example. Gold!!!! For the curious reader of this recommendation - Go to his site now - www.thebucketlistguy.com and subscribe and start working the system - and feel free to share any OTT "pearlers" as you never know they may be shared by myself and others in your network - which is all good - may the forces of positive change be with you ALL!'

Darren Wright – Business Consultant

'I've just wrapped up the three months mentorship programme with Travis Bell, The Bucket List Guy and I have to tell you if you're looking for a place to go where you will meet your peers, and you will be mentored by a fearless leader who will challenge you and teach you all the ins and outs of the public speaking industry as well as challenge you to grow and help you gain insight into your own profession. This is definitely the course for you!'

Emmanuella Grace - Leading voice and performance coach
https://www.emmanuellagrace.com

ENDNOTES

1   Matthews, Gail. "Goals Research Summary". Dominican University of California. Retrieved November 2020. https://www.dominican. edu/sites/default/files/2020-02/gailmatthews-harvard-goals-researchsummary.pdf

2   Pausch, Randy. 'Last Lecture: Achieving Your Childhood Dreams'. Carnegie Mellon University Speech at Carnegie Mellon University, Sept. 18, 2007. https://www.cmu.edu/randyslecture/

3   Ben-Shahar, Tal. *Happier: Can you learn to be Happy?* McGraw-Hill Education, European edition. 16 October 2008

4   The World Bank Organisation, http://www.worldbank.org/

5   The World Factbook 2016-17. Washington, DC: Central Intelligence Agency, 2016. www.cia.gov/library/publications/the-world-factbook/index.html

6   Organisation for Economic Co-operation and Development.

https://data.oecd.org/healthstat/life-expectancy-at-birth.htm

7   Photo by Michael Warren / flickr.com

8   Gallup Business Journal. Robison, Jennifer. "Turning Around Employee Turnover" (Published online, May 8, 2008) Gallup. com. https://news.gallup.com/businessjournal/106912/turning-around-your-turnover-problem.aspx

9   Cigna Neswroom Press Release, (Published online 23 January, 2020). "Cigna Takes Action to Combat The Rise of Loneliness and Improve Mental Wellness in America". www.cigna.com. https://www.cigna.com/newsroom/news-releases/2020/cigna-takes-action-to-combat-the-rise-of-loneliness-and-improve-mental-wellness-in-america

10 Forbes. Bersin, Josh. "New Research Unlocks the Secret of Employee Recognition." (Published online June 13, 2012). https://www.forbes.com/sites/joshbersin/2012/06/13/new-research-unlocks-the-secret-of-employee-recognition/#67f0bf0f5276

11 Gallup. *State of the Global Workplace report*, (2017) Gallup. com. https://www.gallup.com/workplace/238079/state-global-workplace-2017.aspx

12 HRM Consulting. Cachia, John. "Monday.. the most popular day for a "Sickie"." (Published online March 18, 2013). http://hrmconsulting.com.au/_blog/The_World_According_to_Cachia/post/Monday_the_most_popular_day_for_a_Sickie/

13 State of Workplace Mental Health in Australia, TNS Global (www.tnsglobal.com) and Beyond Blue (www.beyondblue.org.au) https://www.headsup.org.au/docs/default-source/resources/bl1270-report---tns-the-state-of-mental-health-in-australian-workplaces-hr.pdf?sfvrsn=8

14 Ibid.

15 Cornerstone OnDemand research report. "Toxic Employees in the Workplace: Hidden Costs and How to Spot Them." (Retrieved 3rd September, 2020). https://www.cornerstoneondemand.com.au/ sites/multisite/files/whitepaper/anz-wp-toxic-employees.pdf

16 Ibid.

Printed in Great Britain
by Amazon